Parenting
by
Faith

What Jesus Said
to Parents

PATRICIA BATTEN

Parenting by Faith: What Jesus Said to Parents

Rose Publishing, LLC
140 Summit Street
P.O. Box 3473
Peabody, Massachusetts 01961-3473
www.hendricksonrose.com

Book cover and layout design by Nancy Bishop and Sergio Urquiza.

ISBN: 978-1-62862-781-7

Printed in the United States of America

010219VP

To the boys whom God has entrusted to us—
Jack, Sam, and Tim—
for the times you refused to change your socks for
weeks on end; for the eight times you broke your
glasses in one year; for the time you rode your
bicycle over the retaining wall.

You increased my faith in God.

You also showed me I could love more than I ever
thought possible. You make my heart sing.

Every single day.

Contents

Introduction

When my ten-year-old son emptied his locker at the end of the school year, he brought home stacks of loose papers, pointless pencils without erasers, a multitude of reusable water bottles, enough granola-bar crumbs to feed our family of five for months on end, and a plastic cup filled with colored beads. We determined which items were destined for the landfill and which would be recycled for new and exciting purposes. I was stuck on the beads.

"What's the cup of beads for?" I asked.

"I won those during class competitions," he said.

"Good job, Jack! You have a lot of beads here. You must have done well," I said with a proud smile.

"Actually…" he began, "the very best students got trophies made by the teacher. The kids who did really well but didn't win first place were given ocean shells. The kids who did so-so got colored rocks. I got beads."

I peered through the plastic cup. I didn't see any shells or colored rocks mixed in with the beads. I swirled the cup with my wrist like I do with my iced coffee. No rocks. No shells.

"Did you get beads *every* time?" I asked.

"No. I got a colored rock *once*," he said while thrusting his hand to the depths of his backpack. He yanked out a shiny white stone.

"My teacher had to give it to me because I was on the winning kickball team. Everyone scored except for me."

An anemic "Oh," was all I could muster. Do you know that "oh"? It's a gut-wrenching, lump-in-your-throat, pit-in-your-stomach "oh" that dribbles off your lips in slow motion.

Jack and I were quiet for a long, exaggerated moment. My hands started sweating. The plastic cup pressed deep into my palm, slipping ever so slightly against my skin.

I knew this mother-son episode could play out in one of two ways: with tears or with laughter. Hoping that my little boy would see the ridiculousness of viewing oneself through the foggy lens of a plastic cup, I tried for laughter by stating the obvious.

Staring into the cup, I broke the ice with a chuckle. I nodded my head and said with raised eyebrows, "That's *a lot* of beads."

He caught on to the absurdity of the situation and laughed. "Yeah, it *is* a lot!" he echoed, with a broad, genuine smile.

Jack saw the humor in this real-life story that sounded more like a plotline ripped out of a tween novel. A bunch of beads can't define us. We laughed. We *really* laughed. I'm grateful that he knows he has strengths in other areas and that he can't be defined by a cup of craft refuse. As a mother in Christ and as a kid in Christ, we both knew that our value comes from Christ alone.

But as a parent, I still had to contend with the sweaty plastic cup filled with beads. I saw a few options. One would have been for Jack to keep the cup of beads on his desk to encourage him to do better next time. Another choice would have been to take the beads and make something better or beautiful out of them—a necklace or a craft stick picture frame. A third alternative would have been to hold a ceremonial "tossing of the beads."

We parents are faced with decisions every day. When our kids come home with a cup of beads, what do we do with them? Is there a *Christian* response? Does the Bible speak to the fears and anxieties of parents?

As a pastor and seminary professor, I've spent a fair amount of time studying the Gospels. Yet I never raised the question, "What does Jesus say to *parents*?" I glanced through the Gospels with fresh eyes and began seeing his interactions with parents scattered among the pages.

In most cases, parents—at their wits' end—approach Jesus in desperate need of his help. These are mothers and fathers who love their children, but their kids are slipping away—because of sickness, disease, or demon-possession. Maybe in your case it's drugs or defiance or a medical diagnosis. Whatever it might be, your child is slipping away.

I've scoured the Gospels in search of uncovering what, if anything, Jesus says to parents when their kids are clenching a handful of colored beads. He speaks very few words, but the words he says are powerful. To a desperate outsider he says, "You have great faith." To a father who struggles with faith, "Everything is possible for one who believes." To the widow of Nain he says, "Don't cry."

But Jesus speaks these words to us, too.

To my surprise, I discovered that the reasons parents approached Jesus in New Testament times are really no different from the reasons why parents approach Jesus today. The specific issues may be different, but the underlying emotions and anxieties, the driving fears, are identical. We're worried about our kids. We want the best for them. We don't know what to do. Or stated another way: We don't know what to do with the beads; we want our kids to have trophies.

There is no record in the Gospels of Jesus ever telling the mothers and fathers *why* their children are suffering. And believe it or not, the parents never raise that question. They simply want Jesus. Maybe that's because when you're standing at the edge of a parenting abyss, you realize that's all you really need. Jesus. He sees. He speaks. He listens. He touches. *He is present among parents.*

After seeing how compassionate Jesus is toward these mothers and fathers in the Gospels, I was surprised at how incredibly loved I felt by the Lord. God cares about parents. God cares about our children. And God still speaks to the needs of mothers and fathers today.

As you read through this book and reflect on the questions at the end of each chapter, my prayer is that you would know that, too: that your trust in the Lord would increase as you begin to comprehend his enormous love for you in this crucial task of parenting. In the process, you might find that you've been carrying around a few beads of your own. My joyful hope is that you'll gain the wisdom to know what to do with the beads and the trophies—and everything in between.

CHAPTER 1

Feasting on Crumbs of Mercy

Matthew 15:21–28

Leaving that place, Jesus withdrew to the region of Tyre and Sidon. A Canaanite woman from that vicinity came to him, crying out, "Lord, Son of David, have mercy on me! My daughter is demon-possessed and suffering terribly."

Jesus did not answer a word. So his disciples came to him and urged him, "Send her away, for she keeps crying out after us."

He answered, "I was sent only to the lost sheep of Israel."

The woman came and knelt before him. "Lord, help me!" she said.

He replied, "It is not right to take the children's bread and toss it to the dogs."

"Yes it is, Lord," she said. "Even the dogs eat the crumbs that fall from their master's table."

Then Jesus said to her, "Woman, you have great faith! Your request is granted." And her daughter was healed at that moment.

What Jesus said to parents:
You have great faith.

Chasing Crumbs

We had ants. Because we had crumbs. We had crumbs. Because we had kids. We got rid of the ants, but we kept the kids and the crumbs. Every parent knows that crumbs are inevitable. But no parent wants them in the house.

We have been blessed with three incredible kids. They're also crumby. Incredibly crumby. We know which child was sitting in which seat just by examining the evidence. Toasted plain bagel with cream cheese is the trademark crumb of the oldest child. Macaroni, cemented to the floor by an orange cheese-like substance, is the work of the middle one. The youngest child leaves behind the most evidence. It's on his seat, around his seat, stuck in the crevices on the table, smashed into the floor, spattered on his face, and strewn throughout his fine locks of yellow hair. He parades through the house, a trail of crumbs falling like fairy dust from the folds of his shirt and pants. I chase crumbs all day long. I could make crumb cake for dinner every night with the morning's dustpan collection.

In Matthew 15, the gospel writer records the plight of a woman who chases after crumbs. But she's chasing and embracing, not sweeping them away.

Why? Because she knows that Jesus can make a feast of mercy out of crumbs. And she's hungry for mercy. Because her life is crumbling.

Jesus' Bite Is Bigger Than His Bark

It's a strange passage in Scripture. We're dealing with demons, dogs, and disciples with deep prejudice. We're looking at bread crumbs and a crummy situation. We're dealing with a broken-hearted, exhausted mother, who begs Jesus for mercy. And then we have a Jesus who doesn't seem to care. The disciples advise Jesus to ignore her. Jesus says his mission is aimed at the lost sheep of Israel, not outsiders. She persists. He insults her. Jesus gives a mother in distress a difficult time. But by the end of the incident, Jesus says to this mother: "You have great faith!"

You read it, and you might feel ashamed. Jesus' words in this passage are tough, shocking. These aren't the words of my Sunday school Jesus. Here's a Gentile—a non-Jewish woman—who desperately needs help, but Jesus says his mission is to help Jews, the chosen children, *not* the two-bit Gentile *dogs* of Syrophoenicia.

It's certainly not my place to advise Jesus. But I want to. I want to tell him to excuse himself from the situation *politely*. No harm done. But don't insult the woman! What are we to make of this bizarre interaction?

Passage Prep for Parents

- Describe a time when you were confused by Jesus or maybe even hurt by other Christians.

- Who might you describe as having great faith?

- The cry for mercy is a prominent refrain in the Psalms, but according to the Gospels, who else cries out for mercy? (For an example, look up Matthew 9:27.)

- There are only two instances in Matthew's gospel in which a woman addresses Jesus. This passage is the first. The other occurs in Matthew 20:20–21 and is made by the mother of James and John. In both instances, a mother takes the initiative in approaching Jesus. Why are both of these instances highly unusual actions for women at the time?

God's Commitment to Mercy: Members Only?

The Israelites were God's chosen people. There was no doubt about that. They were set apart from other nations to follow God and love and worship him alone. Moses said to the assembly: "Out of all the peoples on the face of the earth, the LORD has chosen you to be his treasured possession" (Deuteronomy 14:2). It may sound strange that God would choose one group of people over another, but God's setting apart of the Jews demonstrates his kindness, not his cruelty. God's desire was for a nation that would be a blessing to other nations. When God called Abram and promised to make him into a great nation, God also promised that "all peoples on earth will be blessed through you" (Genesis 12:3).

The Jews were not chosen because of how wonderful they were. They were chosen because of God's mercy: his kindness. So it makes sense that when God became incarnate, he took up flesh and bones among his chosen people in Israel. Jesus' ministry was focused on the Jews. He preached to Jews. He ate with Jews. He healed Jews. *Most of the time.*

Missions of Mercy for Nonmembers

There were occasions in which Jesus ministered to non-Jews, or Gentiles. And whenever a Gentile was healed, Jesus healed *from a distance.*[1] He did it with a word, not a touch.

But this lack of touch didn't mean lack of heart.

The heartbeat of God's mission was among his chosen people in Israel; but here and there, he embarked on a mission of healing and grace into Gentile lives and into Gentile lands, softening the center of hardened heathen hearts. When the time was right, the church would be unleashed to fan those flames and set those souls ablaze for Jesus Christ.

One mission crossed the cultural divide and entered foreign territory. It penetrated the life of a little girl and her desperate mom. It was a mission of mercy.

Mercy for a Mother

And mercy is exactly what this mother needs. She begs Jesus: "Lord, Son of David, have mercy on me! My daughter is demon-possessed and suffering terribly."[2] Have mercy—*on me*. She doesn't say "Have mercy" or "Have mercy on my daughter." This mother needs mercy because watching her child suffer is more than she can handle.

Parents know what it's like to care for someone hard and long, with everything they've got. Mothers in the twenty-first century know why this first-century mom needed mercy.

Mercy for Breaks

When our oldest son was eight years old, we brought him to the doctor to have his legs and feet examined. He was pigeon-toed. Running was a struggle for him, and he often fell for no reason at all. Doctors at Boston Children's Hospital determined that he wasn't pigeon-toed. Instead, he had femoral anteversion. His legs were set at the wrong angle in his hips. I remember the white-knuckled car ride home from the city. I asked, "How do you feel about the diagnosis?" He paused for a moment before replying, "I guess that's why I'm not very good at sports, and I guess that's why I fall a lot. Now at least I know there's a reason."

Femoral anteversion is a condition you can live with. Surgery is elective. But when you're ten years old and you fall in the middle of the hallway at school, or you trip over and over again in front of your peers at gym class, or you're permanently "It" in the game of tag, it becomes a condition you really can't live with.

So…we broke our son's legs. Both of them. Okay, we didn't do it. A surgeon at Boston Children's Hospital did it. But we allowed it. In layman's terms, Jack's legs were crooked. Now they're straight.

I realized right away that I would need mercy to endure his

recovery. Five non-weight-bearing weeks in a wheelchair, followed by another five weeks with the wheelchair, followed by a couple of weeks shuffling around on a borrowed walker with the name *Agnes* imprinted on the front bar, followed by several weeks of leaning on a cane. Yes, he needed mercy. But I needed it, too, because watching a child suffer is absolutely heart-wrenching. And caring for a child with serious needs can leave you drained, dry, and depleted.

Mercy for Brakes

On Jack's first day home from the hospital, we discovered that those levers beneath the wheelchair handles were not, indeed, brakes. Although they looked like they belonged on the handlebars of a child's bicycle, they were, in fact, the complete opposite of brakes. They were release levers. Yes. Release levers. When little brother (toddler Timmy) depressed the "brakes," the back of Jack's seat came crashing down. While Jack was leaning against it, of course.

I needed mercy.

I needed mercy after our first outdoor adventure. It was just one little step to enter the house. My husband said, "Don't worry. I'll pop a wheelie." I gave him one of those dads-are-crazy kind of looks, and I said in a moms-know-everything kind of voice, "I'll just lift the front of the wheelchair a tiny bit to get over the bump." I grabbed hold of the leg rests and lifted, because "pop a wheelie" sounded like something you'd do on a bike with brakes, not a wheelchair with levers. But to my surprise, I learned that those lovely little leg rests actually move when you lift them. Jack's two broken legs got a shocking jolt upward. He screamed. I stepped aside. Rich popped a wheelie. We got in the house.

I was a mom in need of mercy.

Have Mercy on *Me*

The mother in our passage cannot sleep at night. She needs mercy. She doesn't toss and turn in bed, counting sheep. Instead, she counts the number of times her daughter has turned to self-harm. When her daughter screams in fits of rage, contorting her face so that she's unrecognizable, this mother needs mercy. When this little girl withdraws deep within and her stare is hollow, this mother needs mercy. When neighbors and passersby snicker or move to the other side of the road to shield their own *normal* children, this mother needs mercy. When her daughter cries at night because she is confused and scared, this mother needs mercy, because she does not know how to comfort her daughter and make everything okay.

What mother hasn't asked for mercy? She needs the merciful hand of God on her as she raises her little girl. Have mercy on *me*.

Mercy for an Outsider

But she's not asking for mercy as a mother alone. She's asking for mercy as a *Gentile* mother. A non-Jewish woman.

In the Bible, mercy is seen as a quality of God, his kindness lavished on his chosen people. God's mercy meant that

- God faithfully kept his promises
- God maintained his relationship with his chosen people
- God was faithful, even when his people were unworthy and unfaithful

Mercy has to do with his compassion, his loving-kindness. It's the outflow of God's love for his people. God continued to love them, even when they did not deserve it.

But this woman is a foreigner. There is no reason for her to expect mercy. She is not an "approved" recipient of mercy. She's asking for some of the mercy that God bestows on his chosen people. She wants some of the loving-kindness, some of the compassion, some of the pity that God gives to the Israelites. She wants him to act on her behalf. Could she, a Gentile, benefit from the overflow of God's mercy? Were there any crumbs for her? "Have mercy on *me!*" she says. *Me*, a mother. *Me*, a *Gentile.*

The Syrophoenician woman was entrenched in a system of deep-rooted racial prejudice. Her exact experience is not shared by every parent today, but there are ways in which present-day parents feel unchosen, inadequate, living life on the fringes. These parents cry out for mercy:

- "Have mercy on me, a mother with anxiety."

- "Have mercy on me, a father in a messy marriage."

- "Have mercy on me, a parent in financial crisis."

- "Have mercy on me, a single parent."

Not every parent feels a strong sense of "otherness" like the Syrophoencian woman does. But there are some. Many of these parents cry out for mercy in our world:

- "Have mercy on me, an immigrant mother."

- "Have mercy on me, a parent with an addiction."

- "Have mercy on me, the father of a child with special needs."

Mercy for a *Despised* Outsider

This story is recorded in two gospel accounts: Matthew (15:21–28; provided at the beginning of this chapter) and Mark (7:24–30). Both writers want their readers to know loud and clear that this woman is a foreigner and is outside of God's covenant people. People see her as being outside of God's mercy. Mark refers to her as "a Greek, born in Syrian Phoenicia" (verse 26). Matthew chooses the designation "Canaanite" (verse 22)—odd, because, well, there were no Canaanites in New Testament times. In fact, this is the only time the word *Canaanite* is used in the New Testament, though it was often used in the Old Testament.

So why does Matthew use the outdated, seemingly irrelevant term? Because the word *Canaanite* conjured up a certain image and brought back a flood of dismal memories for his audience of Jewish readers. Yes, it meant *foreigner*; but it also meant *enemy*.

When God brought the Israelites into the promised land after Moses died, the land was already inhabited. By Canaanites. God told the Israelites that the Canaanites must go. They worshiped idols. They practiced temple prostitution and were the most sexually depraved religion in ancient times. They even practiced human sacrifice. The first two commandments God gave to his chosen people were in direct opposition to the religion of the Canaanites:

- "You shall have no other gods before me," and

- "You shall not make for yourself an [idol]" (Exodus 20:3–4).

God warned the Israelites against becoming like the Canaanites around them. But their tangible religion of wood and stone carvings proved too much for God's chosen people. They wanted something they could see with their eyes and feel with their hands. And Israel's leaders led them down a path of polytheism, thereby breaking God's commandments.

Parental Hedge Betting

Most of the Israelites didn't deny God, but they added to him. *Just in case.* Just in case God wasn't strong enough; just in case God wasn't kind enough; just in case God wasn't smart enough; just in case God wasn't good enough; just in case God didn't care or wasn't watching; just in case God wasn't sufficient.

They were hedging their bets. Hedges are trees and shrubs that are used as borders in order to limit the size of an area. Over time, the word *hedge* came to refer to *limiting risk*. One way to limit risk was to diversify debt across many lenders instead of being beholden to one single lender.

When we as parents *hedge our bets* with God, we're not trusting him entirely with our children. We're adding to him—just in case. On the outside, this parental addition or diversification may manifest itself as determination, careful planning, information gathering, or perhaps having knowledge of the latest trends and trendsetters and Twitter feeds. Nothing is wrong with thoughtful, knowledgeable, informed parenting. In fact, it's good! Problems arise when on the inside, heart attitudes reveal avoidance of deep trust in God. Fueling our distrust are fears that he is not strong enough, smart enough, good enough, and caring enough.

Searching for the God of Mercy

This Canaanite woman is from a people who worshiped gods unlike the one true God. Canaanite gods were selfish and violent. They were unreliable and untrustworthy. They weren't *real*. And phony gods can't give mercy.

And guess who knows that? This Canaanite woman. She's looking for a God of mercy—for *the* God of mercy. Even though she's not one of the chosen.

When Matthew identifies the woman as a Canaanite, he implies that she's more than a foreigner. She's someone to steer clear of. She is the enemy of ages past. She's dangerous. She's your downfall. Matthew basically says, "Once a Canaanite, always a Canaanite." The disciples don't see a hurting mother; they see an idol-worshiper. Every Jew knew that the Canaanites with their idol worship were the Israelites' downfall, all the way to the exile, so they see her as an enemy. And enemies don't deserve mercy.

Nobody Deserves God's Mercy

But the fact of the matter is, we're all enemies of God. We're all in need of mercy and forgiveness. That mercy hangs on a wooden cross. That mercy rests in the tomb sealed by a cold stone slab. That mercy is a miracle that rises in the dawn on Easter morning. That mercy is the peace treaty signed in the blood of Jesus Christ that says "Forgiven." None of us deserves God's mercy. But he gives it to us just the same.

But the disciples want to dole out stingy doses of God's mercy. They urge Jesus to turn his back on her: "Send her away, for she keeps crying out after us" (verse 23).

Dealing with a Mercy Delay

I can't imagine how difficult it must have been for this mother to continue pursuing Jesus. The crowds surrounding him must have made it clear that she is not welcome. Yet she persists. She needs God's mercy. She needs his kindness in action.

What parent hasn't struggled with God's mercy? We want action. We know he's compassionate, but he doesn't seem to act on our behalf, even when we beg for mercy! We begin to question our pleading. Is there a particular formula for prayer? Are my pleas too long? Too short? Too faithless?

Tight-Petaled Mercy

I remember a hand-painted two-line sign in England, planted in a lush field of green and purple and yellow: "Don't Damage the Daffs / Don't Crush the Crocuses."

Daffodils and crocuses are the harbingers of spring. Don't crush the hope of spring. Don't damage the blossoms of new life. Parenting by faith means there are future blossoms for Christian mothers and fathers whose hope for mercy has been damaged or crushed.

In my New England garden, tulips are the floral forerunners of spring. But in the dead of winter, nothing is in bloom. During one winter cold snap with high temperatures peaking at 10 degrees, Rich surprised me with flowers. He plunged a stiff bundle of yellow tulips inside a blue vase. Their petals were cinched tight by the cold. When I awoke the next morning, the petals were still pursed, unwilling to open and kiss the dawn. Days passed, but the tulips stayed closed. They refused to open even a smidgen and release their sweet, subtle scent. Sometimes I wonder why God won't open up and pour forth the fragrance of his mercy. He's waiting. He's withholding. He's tight-petaled.

Dog as Pet or Dog as Insult?

She wants mercy as a mother. She wants mercy as a Gentile. The disciples don't think she deserves it, and it seems like Jesus doesn't either.

He says, "I was sent only to the lost sheep of Israel" (verse 24).

But there must have been something in his eyes, the look on his face, or his tone that leads this woman to believe Jesus has a crumb for her. Because she persists. She kneels before Jesus and says, "Lord, help me!" (verse 25).

And here's Jesus' startling, embarrassing reply: "It is not right to take the children's bread and toss it to their dogs" (verse 26).

The children, of course, are the heirs, the chosen ones, the Israelites. The dogs…well…they're not. They're Gentiles. They're outside of God's mercy, right? She's a dog, not an heir.

Many scholars are quick to explain that Jesus is not insulting her when he implies that she is a dog. They note that the word Jesus uses for dog is one that means "little dog," so Jesus must be referring to her as a household pet. The implication is that Jesus must take care of the family before he feeds the dog. This makes sense in light of verse 24 where Jesus is recorded as saying "I was sent only to the lost sheep of Israel." He's saying that his mission is first to the chosen people—the Jews. If he went off-mission and started feeding Gentiles, it would be like a father feeding dinner to the family dog while the kids sat hungry at the table.[3] A father's mission is to feed the family first.

But one Middle-East expert, Kenneth Bailey, insists that Jesus did, in fact, *intend* to insult the woman. He argues that Jewish families didn't keep pets in the house.[4] Yes, Jesus softens the insult by describing the dog as "little." But why does Jesus knowingly insult a mother in distress? Maybe this mother knows that Jesus has a larger purpose in mind when he calls her a dog.

Look at her quick response to Jesus: "Yes it is, Lord…[but] even the dogs eat the crumbs that fall from their master's table."

We have two small dogs, both Havanese. Every night around 6:00, they trot to the table and they sit among dangling, fidgety feet, salivating for some juicy morsel to fall to the ground. They are never disappointed. Never. And when a chunk of meatball rolls off the little one's fork, our four-legged friends scoop it up before the poor little boy even realizes he has chomped down on an empty utensil. Disappointment at the table. Delight underneath it. Yes, the dogs have kibble in their dishes, but nothing compares to a home-cooked meal.

This woman is tired of Canaanite kibble. Her religion always leaves her unsatisfied. She is starving for the true God. All this woman wants is a morsel of mercy.

Many of us might hurry off in a huff after Jesus' words. If he's going to heal the girl, just do it already or walk away! Why the talk about Jews and Gentiles, children and dogs? Is he messing with this mother's mind, with her heart and her hopes?

Tightening the Strings of Faith

When brand new strings are placed on a violin or cello, the strings continue to stretch over the next several days, causing the instrument to fall flat in pitch. The violin must be repeatedly retuned. This is known as "break in" time, the time before the strings are settled. A twisting of the tuning peg tightens the string and brings the instrument back into pitch. But strings are vulnerable. If the tuning peg is turned in excess, too much tension will be applied to the string, and it could snap.

Like the concertmaster in a symphony orchestra, Jesus knows this woman is capable of first-chair faith. So he tightens the strings of her faith. *Without snapping them, and without damaging her core.* Her faith will not fall flat. That's what he's doing here. He's applying tension, testing her, pushing her to the limit to see what kind of faith she has. Great tests are given to great students, and she is a great student. Jesus says, "Woman, you have great faith! Your request is granted" (verse 28).

I can picture Jesus speaking these words of mercy to this woman of faith. I can see the two of them in my mind's eye. But the picture is not complete. We've forgotten about the disciples, and we must sketch them into the scene. They got quiet rather quickly. That's because they are not the star students in this episode.

Little Faith—Great Faith

I wonder what Peter in particular thought when he heard Jesus tell the woman she had great faith. I think his heart sank. I know, the passage doesn't tell us that, but take a look at the previous chapter. In Matthew 14:22–36, we're told that the disciples were in a boat on the Sea of Galilee. Jesus stayed behind to pray on a mountainside. It was during the wee hours of the morning while wind whipped fierce fists of water at the wooden vessel. The disciples' eyes were heavy with sleep, so they thought their vision was tricking them. They rubbed their tired eyes. Was it a ghost? No, it was Jesus walking on the water! Peter left the boat and walked toward him. But then Peter took his eyes off Jesus and focused on the wind. Sinking and scared, he screamed, "Lord, save me!" (verse 30). Jesus reached out and caught him. While Jesus was still on the water with Peter clinging to him, Jesus spoke: "You of little faith...why did you doubt?" (verse 31).

Peter, the disciple, had little faith, while a Gentile woman had great faith. I think that's why Peter's heart sank. As soon as he heard Jesus utter the words *great faith* to a woman who he thought deserved to be called a dog, the memory of what happened on the water flooded his mind. It wasn't the cold of the water he remembered. It wasn't the howl of the wind. It wasn't the feeling of sinking and his near death by drowning he recalled. The only thing he remembered was Jesus' voice and those stinging words, *little faith.* The disciple had little faith, and the little dog had great faith.

A Lesson on Mercy

But Peter was learning. They all were learning. They were learning the extent of God's mercy. There are no boundaries. His mercy crosses cultures and creeds, races and religions. It crosses the deepest divides. And all of a sudden, they realized their deep prejudice. They understood why Jesus insulted her by calling her a dog. Jesus never thought of the woman as a dog, but he knew that *they* did. Jesus was demonstrating how ugly their prejudiced thoughts looked when put into action. Kenneth Bailey wrote: "The reference to *dogs* is primarily for the disciples' education. Jesus is saying to them, 'I know you think Gentiles are dogs and you want me to treat them as such! But—pay attention—this is where your biases lead. Are you comfortable with this scene?' "[5]

Jesus doesn't scold them; he doesn't chastise them. He lets the lesson sink in like a refreshing rainfall. The lesson is poured into their souls at just the right pace. Their souls are softer than they were when they first began this journey with Jesus. They are not so hard that a drop of mercy bounces back or a stream of mercy floods them. It's sinking in—that the one they deemed enemy might actually be a friend of God.

Bold Faith

This woman's response is all the bolder because she gives it in front of a gaggle of men who look down on her. Remember what they said to Jesus: "Send her away, for she keeps crying out after us" (verse 23).

Sometimes in this life of parenting, a mother and a father are called to be bold for their children: to make a heart-racing, against-all-odds, stand-your-ground stance. Persisting, even when onlookers glare, because as parents, we know what's best for our children. Moms and dads brush off the needles of the naysayers, and they continue their journey to Jesus. Parents cast aside suspicious stares that whisper, "She doesn't deserve mercy." It's true, we *don't* deserve God's mercy. But neither do they. None of us do. Mercy is God's kindness: the outflow of God's love to undeserving people.

The Canaanite woman doesn't let the antagonistic crowd frazzle her faith. She's undeterred by Jesus' comments. We might pursue some other avenue or get so angry at Jesus that we swear at him or stomp off in anger. But this Canaanite woman knows Jesus has the power to give mercy.

Great Faith and Great Love

Little faith walks away. It says, "Jesus can't do this" or "He doesn't have the time." Little faith says, "I'll just look elsewhere for help" or "Coming to Jesus was a mistake." Little faith turns back, because getting to Jesus was harder than we imagined. A small faith looks at the jeering crowds and is overcome by fear and self-preservation.

But great faith focuses on Jesus and trusts that he has the mercy we need for that moment. Great faith gives parents the strength they need to continue toward Jesus. And when mothers and fathers trust Jesus that much, then everything else becomes background noise. The wind. The waves. The jeering crowds.

What keeps the woman there? Great love and great faith. Great love for her daughter and great faith in Jesus' mercy. She trusts that a crumb from Jesus will change everything. He can make a feast out of crumbs.

Mission of Mercy

Jesus doesn't heal this little girl with a physical touch. He heals her from a distance, in a mission of mercy built on a mother's deep faith.

There are times when God tightens the strings of our faith to the point where we feel we might snap. But he knows the limit of the string. He fine-tunes and tests our faith. And God's mercy is like music that reaches the furthest recesses of the auditorium. His mercy penetrates the regions of race and culture and religion. His mercy is like a melody of hope in an impossible situation.

He releases his mercy at just the right time, from just the right place.

Keep the faith. Keep *great* faith. God has mercy on parents.

Mercy Hatches

By the end of the week, the tulips had been forgotten, and the only fragrance in the house was the smell of taco meat simmering in the pan and permeating every nook and cranny of our home. The kitchen was in full swing, and I was head cook. We topped our shells with mounds of cheese and a heaping side of suppertime insanity. The dogs and the cat played a wild game of tag under our feet. The kids raced back and forth fetching balls and Legos and army men and spelling homework. Rich and I barked out orders to insubordinate soldiers. The scene was uncivilized. We were waiting to hear from the doctor about one of our son's lab results. He had lost eight pounds in three months and complained of belly pain. I wedged an old-fashioned water bottle between the curve of my back and the back of the chair. My back had gone out doing something heroic and meaningful. (Not really. I was sitting in bed and I reached to pull the covers up. My back protested and punished me.) Someone dropped a glass. It was a circus.

Then the red-cheeked little one zoomed by and crashed onto my lap like a wave of fury on an unsuspecting shore. My back jolted. He wagged a pudgy pointer finger in the direction of the blue vase: "Mom, look! Your tulips hatched."

The whir of the carnival circled around me like a carousel, but I couldn't hear it anymore. The flowers had hatched. And that made me smile. I smiled because I loved that he said "hatched." I smiled because he was a red-faced, sweaty bundle of little boy. I smiled because he was aware of what would make me smile. Hatched tulips will always make me smile.

And I remembered that even in the roar of the uproar, tulips still hatch.

When I least expect it, the tulip hatches. And God's mercy blooms.

Measuring Mercy

Sometimes mercy is measured incrementally—in inches rather than miles. Parents want the full measure of mercy in one giant gulp, but God doesn't always drench parents in mercy. Sometimes he delivers it in dollops and dribbles. There's wisdom in taking a mercy measurement to track all of the terrain in which God has provided mercy for parents.

SUMMARY

- God is committed to showing mercy toward his chosen people.

- God also shows mercy to outsiders—non-Jews, or Gentiles.

- Parents need mercy—God's kindness—as they raise their children.

- God tests parents and stretches their faith.

- God's mercy is poured out on people we might think don't deserve mercy.

- Nobody deserves God's mercy; mercy is a gift, not a right that is earned or merited.

- Great faith perseveres toward Jesus and recognizes life's situations and experiences as opportunities to learn and grow.

READ

Psalm 51

TAKE ACTION

Take a mercy measurement by listing the ways in which God has been merciful to you as a parent both in the past and in the present.

PRAY

God of mercy,

Have mercy on me: when I toss and turn at night because I'm worrying about my children; as I make phone calls and craft emails and sit in meetings pertaining to my children; when they cry and I must be strong; when they are discouraged and I must have courage; when my children are full of temper and I must be calm. When I simply don't know what to do, Lord, have mercy. On me. On my children.

Forgive me when I'm impatient with the way you deal with me. Forgive me for not counting the mercies you have given me and continue to give me. Show me how to be a mercy-giver in my home.

Increase my faith in you as I endure my present situation. Thank you for growing me to maturity through the circumstance I now face. When you tighten the strings, be gentle but not so lax that I'm not adequately tested and not so strict that I snap.

I know you love me. I know you love my family. Remind me when I forget.

I pray for _____, parents who so desperately need eyes to see your mercy. Give these parents great faith for the trial they now endure.

Amen.

Questions for Personal Reflection or Group Discussion

1. Describe a situation in which you suffered criticism or mockery when you wholeheartedly advocated for your child.

2. What might inhibit parents from pursuing Jesus or sticking with him?

3. Name several aspects of God's mercy.

4. Who else in Scripture asked for mercy? How is it similar or unlike the woman in this passage?

5. Who else in Scripture did Jesus commend for their faith?

6. Do you think you have more faith now than you did a year ago? Ten years ago? Why?

7. What are some modern examples of people groups that hold prejudices and are at odds like the Canaanites and Israelites were?

8. Measure God's mercy in your life. Have you mainly received big doses of God's mercy in your life, or has his mercy seemed to be given more incrementally? Which would you prefer? Why?

9. Is there anyone who you think doesn't deserve God's mercy? Why?

10. Describe how you are waiting for God's mercy.

11. Do you think your faith has been tested in regard to parenting? What was the result?

12. Identify ways in which you have hedged your bets by adding to God in your present parenting situation.

CHAPTER 2

Parenting without Fear

Mark 5:21–43

When Jesus had again crossed over by boat to the other side of the lake, a large crowd gathered around him while he was by the lake. Then one of the synagogue leaders, named Jairus, came, and when he saw Jesus, he fell at his feet. He pleaded earnestly with him, "My little daughter is dying. Please come and put your hands on her so that she will be healed and live." So Jesus went with him.

A large crowd followed and pressed around him. And a woman was there who had been subject to bleeding for twelve years. She had suffered a great deal under the care of many doctors and had spent all she had, yet instead of getting better she grew worse. When she heard about Jesus, she came up behind him in the crowd and touched his cloak, because she thought, "If I just touch his clothes, I will be healed." Immediately her bleeding stopped and she felt in her body that she was freed from her suffering.

At once, Jesus realized that power had gone out from him. He turned around in the crowd and asked, "Who touched my clothes?"

"You see the people crowding against you," his disciples answered, "and yet you can ask, 'Who touched me?'"

But Jesus kept looking around to see who had done it. Then the woman, knowing what had happened to her, came and fell at his feet and, trembling with fear, told him the whole truth. He said to her, "Daughter, your faith has healed you. Go in peace and be freed from your suffering."

While Jesus was still speaking, some people came from the house of Jairus, the synagogue leader. "Your daughter is dead," they said. "Why bother the teacher anymore?"

Overhearing [or ignoring] what they said, Jesus told him, "Don't be afraid; just believe."

He did not let anyone follow him except Peter, James and John the brother of James. When they came to the home of the synagogue leader, Jesus saw a commotion, with people crying and wailing loudly. He went in and said to them, "Why all this commotion and wailing? The child is not dead but asleep." But they laughed at him.

After he put them all out, he took the child's father and mother and the disciples who were with him, and went in where the child was. He took her by the hand and said to her, "Talitha koum!" (which means, "Little girl, I say to you, get up!"). Immediately the girl stood up and began to walk around (she was twelve years old). At this they were completely astonished. He gave strict orders not to let anyone know about this, and told them to give her something to eat.

What Jesus said to parents:
Don't be afraid.

Plummeting into Fear

In Magic Kingdom Park at Walt Disney World Resort, there's a ride called Splash Mountain. Splash Mountain isn't the fastest ride at the park; it's not the scariest ride either. But there's one heart-stopping moment on the ride that will make you think twice about it. From a lookout point in Frontier Land, spectators have a perfect view of that heart-stopping point of the ride: a 52.5-foot drop, at an angle of about 46 degrees, that each log boat, going 40 mph, must conquer before it meanders around a bend toward safety and the exit.

The five of us stood at the viewpoint and watched as boat after boat took the plunge. Crystals of water shot up like cannons as wooden vessels loaded with screaming passengers thundered downward and popped back up like empty soda cans in a bathtub. By my side a gaggle of boys raised themselves to their tippy-toes and jiggled up and down, yanking on my shorts. "Please, Mom, come on this ride with us!" I had passed on the last ride at Epcot—a simulation into space. Simulations make me sick, but real rides make me scared.

"Okay, let's do it!" I said with false confidence.

Within forty frightful minutes, our Fast Pass had shuffled us to the top of the line. We were about to enter our log float when my husband interrupted the Disney attendant and asked if we could wait for the next boat in order to have the front seat. I don't remember him consulting me on that one.

Aside from a handful of small drops, most of the ride was pretty low-key. But the whole time, I knew what was coming, so I couldn't relax. I sat in fearful anticipation while a freakishly jolly tune "Zip-a-Dee-Doo-Dah"-ed me through the river. After about ten minutes of twists and turns, the vessel made an abrupt stop at the bottom of a huge incline. Fear and dread draped over me in the darkness. Above, vultures warned about my impending doom, and wooden signs cautioned me to turn back. But I knew there was no escape. I was locked into a harness; but even more importantly, I was locked into a pact with my pack of boys.

After the boat in front of us made the plunge, it was our turn to chug to the top. I braced myself, and seconds later, we barreled down the chute like a torpedo.

The photo at the end of the ride portrayed a dismal picture for me personally. My husband and the three wide-eyed boys were grinning, while I had my head buried behind my five-year old. It was embarrassing.

The four of them looked at me and chided, "Why were you so afraid?"

Do Not Be Afraid

That's a question that comes up twice in Mark's gospel. When the disciples were bandied about in a wooden boat in the midst of a terrifying storm, Jesus asked them why they were afraid (Mark 4:35–40). It seems like a silly question.

Later, in Mark 5, Jesus says to a frightened father, "Do not be afraid," even though the man's daughter has just died.

In each of these cases, fear seems to me to be a very appropriate response.

But Jesus doesn't want parents to live in fear. He wants them to live in faith.

Passage Prep for Parents

- What do you fear as a parent?

- In Mark 5:41, we're told that Jesus took the little girl by the hand and told her to stand up. What other young person does Jesus raise from the dead and tell to get up (Luke 7:14)? Do you think that's an important detail? Why or why not?

- Compare and contrast Jairus and the woman with the issue of blood:

  ☙ How old is Jairus's daughter?

- How many years has the woman suffered?

- According to Mark 5:23, Jairus asks Jesus to do what?

- What does the woman do to obtain healing (verse 28)?

- What is Jairus's association with religion (verse 22)?

- Read Leviticus 15:25–31. What is the woman's relationship to organized religion and worship due to her condition (Mark 5:25)?

- How does Jesus address the woman (verse 34)?

Drawing Your Fears

When I was teaching a lower elementary Sunday school class, the curriculum called for the kids to draw a picture of something they feared. Every child was handed an index card on which they colored big hairy spiders and monsters at night and wolves with sharp teeth. We made a house of cards with our fears, and we learned that fear is no match for faith in the one true God. The house of fears came crashing down.

Nobody has asked me to draw my fears lately, but I wonder what a group of parents might create if given index cards and a few colored pencils. Long gone are the fears of spiders and midnight monsters and sharp-toothed howlers under a misty moon. They've been replaced by adult fears. Maybe some might draft a dollar sign or portray a pink slip; others might depict a wedding band or color the curve of a broken heart or sketch the rod of Asclepius, the snake winding around a staff, symbolizing the medical profession; perhaps others might draw a gun next to a school or a hashtag with the words *me too*. But I think most parents would draw their children. Parents fear for their kids.

We fear for their safety: their falls and foibles and failures.

According to Mark, Jairus's greatest fear just about to become a reality: his child will die.

We don't know the nature of the little girl's illness. Did it come on quickly? Is it something she was born with? All we know is that Jairus comes to Jesus at the last possible moment. The girl is about to die.

Scripture never tells us that Jairus delayed his decision to see Jesus or was prodded by his wife to go to Jesus; but certainly, going to Jesus was indeed risky business for Jairus. After all, he was a respected leader in the synagogue. All eyes were on him.

SCRIPTURE INSIGHT

Synagogues were a big deal in Jesus' day. There were hundreds of them scattered throughout the land, and they provided the venue for weekly worship. The Temple, on the other hand, was located in Jerusalem, and it was the place where sacrifices were offered. Israelites made pilgrimages to the Temple three times a year to celebrate required festivals, like the Passover, but a synagogue could be found in most major towns. Some scholars say there were no fewer than four hundred and eighty synagogues in the city of Jerusalem during the time of Jesus.[6]

Faithful Jews and Gentiles who wanted to learn more about God—both men and women—attended Sabbath services each week at their local synagogue. Scripture was read and explained. Prayers were lifted to heaven.

A leader in the synagogue was responsible for planning the weekly worship service and caring for and maintaining the building. He invited people to preach and explain God's Word. He decided who read Scripture and who gave the benediction. The synagogue leader was a big deal in the community.

Workplace Fear

As a synagogue leader, Jairus enjoyed his position and prestige in the community. All of that could be at risk if the religious leaders realized that Jairus had aligned himself with Jesus.

Jairus's family might lose their standing in the community's religious life. When they went to synagogue, they probably got the best bench in the house—maybe the one closest to the box that held the Scriptures, the Torah ark.[7] Or maybe they had an unobstructed view of the service leader, while others with lower social status craned their necks and bobbed side to side in order to catch a glimpse between the imposing columns.

Fear Can Prevent Parents from Going to Jesus

But trusting Jesus meant more than the potential loss of position and prestige. It was downright dangerous. The Pharisees had already made an unlikely coalition with the Herodians. Herodians were Jews who had cozied up to King Herod and the oppressive rule of Rome. Typically, Pharisees and Herodians didn't get along. But both groups were after the same thing: the death of Jesus. These enemies joined forces to form a fearsome front against Jesus. Their goal was to figure out how to kill Jesus without upsetting the masses who were flocking to him (Mark 3:6). They began a slander campaign that gained traction when religious leaders in Jerusalem accused Jesus of being in league with the devil. Would Jairus run to the man whom his superiors accused of working alongside Satan? Did Jairus really want to align himself with the man whom powerful religious leaders wanted to kill? Going to Jesus was not an easy decision for Jairus. He had much to lose. He had much to fear.

But his greatest fear was losing his daughter.

Faith Is Trust with Thrust

So Jairus takes a step of faith. He trusts that Jesus has the power to save his daughter. Faith is trust with thrust. It gets us moving toward Jesus, *despite our fear.* Jairus moved from inaction to action because he trusted that Jesus had power over his fears.

This father in distress hears that Jesus has just returned from the other side of the lake. He's in Capernaum. This is Jairus's last chance. The girl is fading fast. It's do or die. Maybe his wife pleads with him to find Jesus and presses him while they stand in the courtyard of their home. Her face streaked by a river of salt that has flowed over to the folds of her garment, she buries her head in a sea of despair. A muffled cry begs her husband to *please* find Jesus.

He bolts into the street. Fear immobilized him, but faith makes him fly. He stops for no one. No greetings. No *shaloms.* "Is that Jairus, the synagogue ruler?" merchants whisper as a blur kicks up dust and darts down toward the water.

SCRIPTURE INSIGHT

Why did the religious leaders have murderous intentions, especially when Jesus was doing so much good?

Jesus was often invited to preach in synagogues. On one such occasion, he entered the synagogue in Capernaum and was met by a demon-possessed man. Jesus cast out the demon. The people were amazed by Jesus' teaching and by his power over evil spirits (Mark 1:21–28). On another occasion, Jesus healed a man with a withered hand (Mark 3:1–6) and on still another, a woman with a crooked back (Luke 13:10–17). The Gospels tell us that Jesus often taught and healed in synagogues (Matthew 4:23; 9:35; John 18:20).

But Jesus' teaching and healing in the synagogues caused a stir among religious leaders. His ministry in the synagogues whipped up a storm of anger. Religious leaders began fetching ingredients to concoct a deadly recipe.

Two chapters before we read about Jairus, Jesus performed a miracle of healing. He did it in a synagogue on the Sabbath. What better time, what better place, one might ask? But according to some Pharisees, like those who adhered to the school of Shammai, a strict interpretation of the law led them to believe that healing on the Sabbath was a sin. Pharisees who belonged to the school of Hillel were on the other end of the spectrum and were more lenient in their interpretation of the law. They often made their decisions based on the welfare of everyday people. For them, healing on the Sabbath was a good thing, because it showed love and concern for people.

The Talmud, a body of writing comprised of Jewish history and law and its application to life, tells the story of a Gentile who wanted to convert to Judaism. He went to Shammai and asked to be taught the entire Torah while he stood on one foot. Shammai was insulted by the ridiculous request. The Gentile then went to Hillel and asked the same question. Hillel replied, "That which is hateful to you, do not do to your fellow man. That is the whole Torah. The rest is commentary; go and learn" (Shabbat 31a). Jesus turned Hillel's words from the negative to the positive when he issued his version of the

Golden Rule: "Do to others what you would have them do to you, for this sums up the Law and the Prophets" (Matthew 7:12).

It's most likely that Jesus was at odds with Pharisees who followed the school of Shammai. According to them, healing was considered work. Wanting to honor God on the Sabbath by keeping it holy as the fourth commandment requires, these Pharisees saw Jesus as one who blatantly disregarded all that they held dear. The Pharisees and other religious leaders who were present got so angry, they began to plot Jesus' death, because in their eyes, Jesus was a lawbreaker. He was working—healing—on the Sabbath. Jesus was also gaining glory among the people, and the religious leaders were losing it. And none of the Pharisees or religious leaders liked that one bit.

Their slander campaign gained traction when religious leaders in Jerusalem accused Jesus of being in league with the devil: "He is possessed by Beelzebul! By the prince of demons he is driving out demons" (Mark 3:22).

It's not hard to spot Jesus. Throngs of people surround him at the water's edge. Jesus is hemmed in, but Jairus snips the seam with the sharp edge of a fearless faith and a father's love. The crowd unfolds. It opens up like the Red Sea, and Jairus casts himself at the feet of Jesus.

"My little daughter is dying. Please come and put your hands on her so that she will be healed and live" (verse 23).

Here's a man who has position and power. He is known. People listen to him. But according to Mark, we find him lying prostrate with his face planted in the sand, begging Jesus to listen to him.

Children can bring us to our knees, can't they?

Jesus Answers the Call

And "Jesus went with him."

That one phrase—"Jesus went with him" (verse 24)—is loaded with relief and gratitude. Everything will be okay because Jesus is going with him. Jairus didn't have to fear that he had made the wrong decision in going to Jesus. It had been the right thing to do. Jesus was coming with him, and his daughter will be okay.

This parent feels relief. It's that just-in-the-nick-of-time kind of relief. He has made it. *Phew!* He can release the breath that had been imprisoned in his chest. The adrenaline that had coursed through his veins at breakneck speed slows down, because he has gotten to Jesus in time.

Dealing with Delay

But Jairus quickly realizes that the walk back to his home won't be a walk in the park. His chest tightens again as the force of the crowd closes in. Jesus isn't the only one going back to Jairus's home. The two men are accompanied by a crushing crowd—bumping and jostling and squeezing tight. They want to see a miracle.

But this is more than a spectacle for Jairus. This is his daughter. Like a herdsman, he drives the people on. But they are slow and stubborn and soon come to a complete halt when Jesus asks who touched him.

It's a silly question, really. The disciples even admit that. They say, "You see the people crowding against you…and yet you can ask, 'Who touched me?'" (verse 31).

I can only imagine what Jairus is feeling now. He must want to prod, poke, and push Jesus forward, toward the *true* destination.

But sometimes our goal isn't the same as God's, and sometimes he wants to teach us something along the way. From our perspective, his timing seems off. His priorities are confusing. He delays in getting where he should be.

But in that delay, God demonstrates his kindness to one who suffers silently. And in that delay, there is something to learn.

Jairus's story comes to an abrupt halt. He is now part of the crowd. He's not the main event. We're told nothing of his reaction, but his faith must be hanging by a thread. His fear ties knots in his stomach and picks at the slender stitch of faith that holds him together. As Jesus patches a frayed and fragile woman, Jairus's life unravels. But will his faith stay intact?

Stopping for the Silent Sufferer

Now our eyes are focused on someone who looks nothing like the respected leader of the synagogue. Jairus is a man; she is a woman. He is respected; she is ignored. He makes his plea for help publicly; she does it privately. He is in charge of the synagogue; she's not allowed in it. He is clean; her sickness makes her unclean.

But with one touch of Jesus' robes, the woman with the prolonged issue of blood is healed.

Not a Bedtime Story for Children

Every night when we put the kids to bed, we read a Bible story. We often read from a children's book of Bible stories, but sometimes we read directly out of the Bible. One week, Rich came home late a few nights, so I did the story on my own. I read the kids this one, from Mark 5, because I had been working on it during the day. I figured it would be a nice change of pace from David and Goliath, or Daniel and the lions' den.

You should have heard the response I got from my three little ones when I read that this woman had been bleeding for twelve years. They were picturing some sort of zombie—a Halloween-type figure who had blood pouring out of her head and her face and her fingertips and her feet. They imagined a woman spattered with scrapes and scratches and an assortment of boo-boos and bandages covering her body. Decades distant from a child's pre-adolescent ignorance of menstruation, I said with a chuckle, "No, it wasn't like that. She wasn't bleeding all over."

"Where was she bleeding?" they asked.

Now I was the zombie, staring at them with an empty gaze. Maybe a more squeamish parent might have said, "She was bleeding out of her nose. She had chronic nosebleeds." Instead, I went right ahead and gave those incredulous children the truth.

My husband was on time the next night. Proper education in physiology aside…we were all grateful.

A Scrap of Faith Saves Life

It has an almost magical quality to it, doesn't it? Steal away with a secret touch and snatch the power. But Jesus makes it publicly clear that there's no magic involved. She's healed by *his* power. Mark tells us in verse 30: "At once Jesus realized that power had gone out from him." And his power is released not by touch but by trust. Jesus tells the woman that her *faith* has healed her. She had believed that Jesus had the power to heal.

But let's face it, she doesn't have *great* faith like the Canaanite woman described in Matthew 15. The fabric of this woman's faith was of a poor quality—weaved with thin threads of a weak theology. She thinks she can syphon Jesus' power with a hocus-pocus touch, without ever talking to him. She doesn't have a great *stack* of faith. But she does have a *scrap* of faith. And this scrap of faith saves life. In fact, the word for *heal* is often translated "saves." When Jesus says, "Daughter, your faith has *healed* you," the word *healed* could easily be translated *saved*: "Daughter, your faith has *saved* you" (verse 34). Jesus does not save apart from faith. Even if it's only a scrap of faith.

The woman trusts that Jesus has the power to heal. And that's enough faith. Jesus doesn't allow her to slink silently back into the folds of the crowd. Instead, he commends her faith and pronounces her clean *in public.*

But first, she had to tell the whole truth.

Telling the Whole Truth

"Then the woman, knowing what had happened to her, came and fell at his feet and, trembling with fear, told him the whole truth" (Mark 5:33).

As parents, we know that there's "the truth" and then there's "the *whole* truth."

Most arguments between my children happen when I'm downstairs and they're upstairs, or I'm cooking and they're playing. I dash into the family room or the bedroom and ask, "What happened?" The carnage is everywhere. I access my mental clipboard as I assess the damage. There are three men down. One is groaning; another one, crying; a third one, defiantly defending himself. I see a splotch of red on a scrawny arm that's been squeezed and yanked. Glasses are on the floor next to the lamp that used to be on the bureau.

I identify equipment failures. A green army guy dangles from the ceiling fan. His parachute did not deploy. A smashed-up Lego starship is scattered across the bedroom galaxy. I attribute that to enemy fire. The bunk-bed ladder is napping horizontally on the ground. Surely a tactical maneuver. "Who's in charge here?" I shout like an angry general. All is quiet on the bedroom battlefield. I fear that I am the one in charge, and I have no idea what to do.

Then the troops gain their courage, and that's when I get many different "truths." "He pushed me." "He wrecked my Lego set." "He wouldn't let me play." "He took my First Order Storm Trooper."

But the *whole* truth tells about *all* of the battles that led up to the war. The *whole* truth helps us understand how we got to that particular moment in time. The *whole* truth is more than the facts. It's feelings and fears and frustrations. The *whole* truth is what Jesus wants to hear. It's our story.

Sometimes the whole truth is hard to tell. Even so, Jesus wants to hear it, because he is interested in healing the *whole* person.

The Whole Truth about Suffering

What was the whole truth that the unnamed woman told Jesus? Mark told us in verses 25 and 26: "A woman was there who had been subject to bleeding for twelve years. She had suffered a great deal under the care of many doctors and had spent all she had, yet instead of getting better she grew worse."

When she tells Jesus the whole truth, she tells him that she had a bleeding condition. She tells him about the money she had wasted on feckless and reckless doctors. She tells him that she had spent all she had. She is poor. We don't know the names and faces of these doctors, but she will never forget them. Perhaps a local doctor in Capernaum sent her to a specialist in Sepphoris. Then maybe on to Jerusalem or on a wild goose chase into the country to visit a doctor who prescribed herbal medicine that helped a friend of a friend of a friend. She tells Jesus that she had tried everything. Elixirs and salves, oils and ointments and exercises. She had been under the care of doctors but to no avail. None of the advice, none of the medicine,

> The gospel writer Luke, who himself was a doctor, does not include the detail that the woman actually grew worse under the care of physicians.

47

cured her problem. In addition to emptying her purse, it actually had made her condition worse.

She has nothing left to give financially. Nothing left to give physically. Nothing left to give emotionally. She tells Jesus the whole truth. She tells him that she touched him because she wants healing.

No Purity, No Peace

This unnamed woman tells Jesus the whole truth about her twelve-year-old bleeding condition *in front of a large crowd*. The crowd must have cringed and engaged in a collective gasp and automatically stepped back away from the unclean woman. The woman wasn't dirty the way our kids are dirty after a romp in the sandbox or a trek through the woods. The law specified that certain things could make a person unclean and not fit for worship. Some of those things were quite natural, ordinary parts of life, like giving birth or burying the dead.[8]

"When a woman has her regular flow of blood, the impurity of her monthly period will last seven days, and anyone who touches her will be unclean till evening.... Whether it is the bed or anything she was sitting on, when anyone touches it, they will be unclean till evening." (Leviticus 15:19, 23)

But this woman could not get into a sustained state of purity...for twelve years. She was always impure, always unclean. That was the ritual effect of chronic bleeding. But imagine the physical effect of chronic bleeding. Certainly, she was anemic. Pale and weak. Then there were the social consequences of her condition. People didn't want to be around her, because they could become impure and unclean by association.

There were also religious implications. She was not permitted to enter the synagogue or the Temple. When the rest of her relatives and community made their pilgrimage to Jerusalem three times a year for festivals, she stayed behind. Every time. For twelve years. The quiet was so intense it was deafening.

Because she had no access to the Temple, she had no access to God. She had no peace with God. She yearned to hear the priestly benediction that told her God was not angry: "Go in peace."

Trembling with the Truth

She trembles as she spills the whole truth out to the Savior. Her secret touch of healing is now exposed to a multitude of people. Will the crowd turn against her? Will Jesus be angry? After all, she just made him—and possibly scores of bystanders—unclean. Will he take her healing away?

That's why the woman in our passage *trembled with fear* when she fell at Jesus' feet. How would Jesus treat her whole truth? Everyone else she had asked for help took advantage of her whole truth or ignored her whole truth or increased her pain. But not Jesus. Women can trust Jesus with the whole truth.

Jesus doesn't recoil. Instead, he calls her *"Daughter."* It's the only time Jesus refers to someone as "daughter" in Scripture. *The only time.* Right here. He reserves the word for this silent sufferer who secretly threads her way through the crowds to him and then must publicly proclaim her whole truth. She does it all on a scrap of faith. *Daughter* is a tender term of endearment and love. It's a word that says you are family, you belong.

Confused by Jesus

Notice that Jesus does not send her to a priest to be pronounced clean. Instead, Jesus himself pronounces her clean in front of the entire assembly: "Go in peace and be freed from your suffering" (verse 34).

One can only imagine what Jairus is thinking. He has concerned himself with purity and religious rituals; but here, Jesus' actions are contrary to Jairus's understanding of religion:

- Jesus requires no sacrifice from the woman.
- She is not reprimanded for making scores of people in the crowd unclean.
- Jesus, not a priest in a holy place, declares her to have peace with God.

Jesus has given her lasting physical healing ("be freed from your suffering"), but he's also given her something more: peace. When a priest spoke the words "Go in peace," he would have referred to peace with God that results in peace with others.

Yes, she has physical healing, but she has gained so much more. This woman's touch of faith has given her a relationship with Jesus. She trusts him. Now she has peace with God.

One daughter who has been sick for twelve years has been healed. But there's still another twelve-year-old daughter who remains in a desperate, even deadly, situation.

Trusting Jesus in the Midst of Fear

No sooner does Jesus pronounce the woman clean than a band of grave faces approach Jairus. His daughter, they tell him, is dead. They advise Jairus not to bother Jesus any longer (verse 35). Some commentators believe the thrust of the heralds' comments are loaded with sarcasm and cynicism. Instead of "Why bother the teacher anymore?" meant in a courteous, considerate way, it's meant in a disrespectful manner. What the messengers really mean is "Why did you ever go to him in the first place?"

When our greatest fears are realized, it's easy to lose hope. That's the time when people walk away, because God didn't prevent it; he didn't stop it. We listen to the grave naysayers surrounding us: "You stuck with Jesus, and he let you down. You're a fool to stay with him! It was a mistake to follow him in the first place."

But Jesus wastes no time in telling Jairus not to be afraid, even though his greatest fear has come true. Jesus wants Jairus to keep on believing that Jesus can save—even in an impossible situation.

Jairus trusts that going to Jesus and staying with him in faith, despite an impossible situation, is the right decision.

He ignores the grave messengers, and he clings to Jesus.

The human father and the Son of God march back to the home where the daughter lies dead. Professional mourners are already on the scene, weeping and wailing, making a commotion. Jesus dismisses them—but not before he tells them the girl is not dead but asleep.

Of course, the little girl is indeed dead. Both Matthew's and Luke's accounts confirm this. Jesus means that her death is the kind that won't last. It's the kind of death that can turn to life again. Everyone laughs at Jesus.

Jairus and his wife accompany Jesus, Peter, John, and James to the girl's room. Will these parents' hopes be dashed once more? They put their trust in Jesus, and their faith triumphs over their fear. Jesus holds her hand and says, "Little girl, I say to you, get up!" (verse 41). Without hesitation, the girl stands up and walks around (verse 42).

Then her parents feed her. An appetite is a sign of life and health. The daughter is alive!

SCRIPTURE INSIGHT

In this story, Jesus' closest followers get an exclusive backstage pass to the supreme miracle: a resurrection. Peter, John, and James will be singled out on another occasion: A Father-Son mountaintop experience. On the mountaintop, the three disciples were given a front row seat to Jesus' glory (Mark 9:2–13). A few chapters later, the three plus Andrew were described as receiving private teaching from Jesus about the end times (Mark 13:3–37). Finally, this inmost circle was on the front lines in the garden of Gethsemane when Jesus was in deep distress and overwhelmed by sorrow (Mark 14:33).

Peter, James, and John were set apart to be with Jesus during special moments of revelation. When Mark wrote about the twelve disciples whom Jesus appointed, he was sure to include the fact that three of the disciples received nicknames from Jesus. These three were listed first: "These are the twelve he appointed: Simon (to whom he gave the name Peter), James son of Zebedee and his brother John (to them he gave the name Boanerges, which means "sons of thunder"), Andrew, Philip, Bartholomew, Matthew, Thomas, James son of Alphaeus, Thaddaeus, Simon the Zealot and Judas Iscariot, who betrayed him" (Mark 3:16–19).

While giving these men special insight into who he was, Jesus prepared these men for future ministry and sacrifice. But maybe even more than that, Jesus revealed his humanity as he shared significant parts of his life and mission—the unbounded joys and the deepest sorrows—with three close friends.

Jairus trusted Jesus with his greatest fear, and Jesus did the impossible.

We're not told what happens next in the life of this family. But I imagine life was never the same.

Imagining the Future

If Jairus keeps his job at the synagogue, he will be a better leader. He'll have eyes for people he never noticed before. Imagine the scene: The very next Sabbath, the unnamed woman from the crowd walks through the door to the synagogue. She hasn't been to a worship service in twelve years! She's clean. She has peace with God. Jairus greets her and asks for her name. At one time, Jairus saw her as the reason for his daughter's death. She was the delay he pushed past in the crowd. Now he sees her as the reason for his daughter's resurrection, and he will never forget her.

Parenting by faith means bringing fears to Jesus with the knowledge that his power is at work in impossible situations. Going to Jesus in our fear, *with* our fear, is always the right thing to do. Faith triumphs over fear.

When we take a look at Mark's gospel, we see a painting of a Jesus who has power over the spiritual realm, as evidenced by the casting out of the demon in Mark 1. He has power over nature, as seen in the calming of the storm (Matthew 8:23–27; Luke 8:22–25). He has power over sickness, as the unnamed woman and countless others experienced. And Jesus has power over death.

What are we afraid of as parents? What keeps us up at night? Have we built a house of fears? Our house of fears can't stand when we have faith in Jesus, because his power is at work in the most fearsome situations.

Battling Fear

When our youngest was only three weeks old, I loaded him in the car along with his three-year-old brother. It was our first trip outside of the house since he was born. We were off to a specialty food store. This wasn't major grocery shopping. I simply wanted to grab a handful of items that my local grocery chain didn't offer. I really just wanted to get out of the house. But I was tired. So tired. The baby was, too, because he slept for the twenty-five-minute ride.

The parking lot was hopping, and I was lucky to get a space. I unlatched the baby seat and hooked my right arm through the handle. I always feared the transition from car to store, but the baby didn't wake up. My three-year-old held my hand as we crossed the parking lot with cars darting off in all directions. The sun was shining, and it felt good to be outside. I pulled forward the little front seat of the shopping cart and plunked the infant carrier in the larger basket area. The cart was on the smaller side, so the infant seat fit snugly. I'd have to put any groceries in the shelf under the cart. The baby was still fast asleep.

We meandered through the store and ended up in the dairy section. The yogurt caught Sam's eye. I parked the grocery cart right behind me, and Sam and I reviewed the possible yogurt selections: orange, strawberry, lemon, lime, or cherry. Sam didn't really start talking until he was over the age of two, but his language started to blossom by age three. He repeated the flavors after me, and I loved hearing that sweet voice. He pointed to the container with the picture of two plump, ripe strawberries. I grabbed a couple and reached back for the cart.

But it wasn't there.

I can't remember a more fearful moment in motherhood.

There are no words to describe what I felt. In fact, my heart is racing as I write this. Did I leave the cart in Produce? Was my baby by the bananas? No. The shopping cart had been with me. I was sure of it.

Sam and I dashed through Dairy and Produce. Nothing. We raced to the first aisle in the store. Not there. In the second aisle, halfway down, was a woman rushing toward the front of the store.

"That's my cart!" I yelled. I sprinted to the cart and grabbed hold of it. "You have my baby!"

She rattled off an explanation about accidentally grabbing the wrong shopping cart. I was suspicious. I remember telling her that once upon a time I too had accidentally taken the wrong cart—but never one with a baby in it!

I left the store visibly shaken. Cars rushed past me. I had a tight grip on Sam's hand, and the baby carrier was cradled under my right arm. He was still sleeping. I cried. If her intentions had indeed been evil, thirty more seconds would have given her the opportunity to exit the store and disappear into a crowded parking lot. With my baby.

It's a parent's worst fear. But even after he was safe in my arms, I still wrestled with fear. I was obsessed with locking our doors and windows. In addition to the locks and bolts, I placed a chair under the doorknob. When the baby moved into the nursery, I got up twice a night for two years to make sure he was still there. I believed any thump or bump in the night would end in tragedy. Living with my fear was *exhausting*.

I told Jesus the whole truth. I confessed that I feared I was a bad mother. I told him how I couldn't sleep. I told him how I feared it would happen again. I told him how I woke my husband up with every noise in the night. I told him how I was afraid to go out with the kids alone. I told him how I was tired and cranky. I told him how I didn't know what I would have done if I had lost my son. I told Jesus the whole truth.

And I remembered Scripture. I have a relationship with God through Jesus Christ. I am a child of God. He calls me *"Daughter."* That means that tender word that Jesus used only once in the New Testament, he uses for *me*. Every single day. I am his daughter. I belong to him, and he will take care of me. I hear him say, "Don't be afraid. Keep on trusting." Even when my greatest fear has been realized, I must keep trusting God. Because he can do the impossible, even in the most fearsome event that life flings my way.

Daughter, don't be afraid. Keep on trusting in Jesus.

SUMMARY

- As a synagogue leader, Jairus had a lot to lose in going to Jesus.
- Fear can prevent us from going to Jesus.
- Faith is trust with thrust. Faith keeps us moving toward Jesus despite our fears.
- God's seeming delay is an opportunity for our faith to be tested and strengthened.
- Jesus responds to a scrap of faith.
- Jesus wants us to tell him the whole truth, so he can wholly heal us.
- Jesus gives us peace when we trust in him.

READ

Psalm 23

TAKE ACTION

Watch *The Miracle Maker* with your children.

PRAY

Dear God,

Today my fear for my children is _____. When I think about it too much, fear sets in and sinks its claws right into my soul. Help me to trust you with this. I want to see your glory in this situation.

Help me not to delay in bringing you my worries and anxieties. When it seems that you delay in answering me, give me patience and the ability to lean into the pause and learn.

I admit that my own circumstances have blinded me to the plight of other people's pain. Give me eyes to see those I don't normally notice. Help me to see how they might be suffering, and allow me to see your work in their lives.

I pray for daughters (and sons), both young and old, who need your healing touch. Some need to tell you the whole truth because they've bottled it up inside for years. They need to hear you say, "Go in peace." Some need relief from suffering. I pray that you will give it to them.

I pray for children who struggle with fear and anxiety. Some can't sleep at night. Some bite their nails or pick at their skin till it turns red and raw. I lift up _____ to you, God. Help them not to be afraid.

Why little ones would ever be knocking at death's door is beyond me. I don't understand it. But I trust you. Turn weeping and wailing into dancing.

Amen.

Questions for Personal Reflection or Group Discussion

1. What do you fear for your child today?

2. Has fear ever prevented you from running to Jesus? Maybe fear of what others—a colleague, a spouse, a family friend, or a parent—might think? Explain.

3. Describe a time in which you ended up at Jesus' feet, pleading with him on behalf of your children, "Come, Jesus. Come now!"

4. Think of a time when you asked, "Why are we stopping here, God?"

5. What whole truth do you have to bring to Jesus?

6. Think of a truth that has left you feeling like you have nothing left to give financially, physically, or emotionally.

CHAPTER 3

Everything Is Possible with God

Mark 9:14–32

When they came to the other disciples, they saw a large crowd around them and the teachers of the law arguing with them. As soon as all the people saw Jesus, they were overwhelmed with wonder and ran to greet him.

"What are you arguing with them about?" he asked.

A man in the crowd answered, "Teacher, I brought you my son, who is possessed by a spirit that has robbed him of speech. Whenever it seizes him, it throws him to the ground. He foams at the mouth, gnashes his teeth and becomes rigid. I asked your disciples to drive out the spirit, but they could not."

"You unbelieving generation," Jesus replied, "how long shall I stay with you? How long shall I put up with you? Bring the boy to me."

So they brought him. When they spirit saw Jesus, it immediately threw the boy into a convulsion. He fell to the ground and rolled around, foaming at the mouth.

Jesus asked the boy's father, "How long has he been like this?"

"From childhood," he answered. "It has often thrown him into fire or water to kill him. But if you can do anything, take pity on us and help us."

"'If you can'?" said Jesus. "Everything is possible for one who believes."

Immediately the boy's father exclaimed, "I do believe; help me overcome my unbelief!"

When Jesus saw that a crowd was running to the scene, he rebuked the impure spirit. "You deaf and mute spirit," he said, "I command you, come out of him and never enter him again."

The spirit shrieked, convulsed him violently and came out. The boy looked so much like a corpse that many said, "He's dead." But Jesus took him by the hand and lifted him to his feet, and he stood up.

After Jesus had gone indoors, his disciples asked him privately, "Why couldn't we drive it out?"

He replied, "This kind can come out only by prayer."

What Jesus said to parents:
Everything is possible for one who believes.

Picture-Perfect Parenting

We have a large framed photograph hanging on our wall in the mudroom. It's a picture of two of the boys, taken in front of Nubble Lighthouse in York, Maine, before we had our third son. It's the first thing you see upon entering our house, and it's the last thing you see upon leaving. The verse below the picture, Matthew 5:14, says: "You are the light of the world." I want my kids to remember that when they live as followers of Jesus Christ, they are lights in a dark world.

I also love this picture because it reminds me of a perfect day we had with the boys. I know, there are no perfect days; but this one came close. We packed some sandwiches and snacks and headed north on Interstate 95. We didn't leave our house until after Sam's 1:00 nap, so we missed the summer traffic. We scored a parking space alongside the village green. I spread out the picnic blanket on the neatly manicured lawn. A concert was in progress. In the gazebo, a band played tunes of a bygone era while our kids danced, tickling the grass with their toes. The Atlantic Ocean was the backdrop to their performance: the crashing waves, their applause. We tossed around a ball; devoured ice cream cones; played skee ball. A gentle ocean breeze swept away the nuisance of mosquitoes. Nobody cried; nobody complained; nobody fought; nobody threw up or got a rash. At the end of our day, I snapped a picture of the two boys nestled in the rocks in front of Nubble Light. They both smiled generous grins—wide and toothy. At the same time.

It was a perfect day.

Then we packed up the van. Our perfect day faded away in the rearview mirror as the sun dipped deep below the horizon. We stumbled into a dark home, each bearing a bundle of sleepy little boy. We wove our way through a minefield of stray toys. There were dishes to wash, clothes to clean, dogs to walk, phone calls and emails to return, numbers to crunch, and lessons to prepare.

Farewell, picture-perfect parenting; back to reality.

SCRIPTURE INSIGHT

Although Matthew and Mark don't mention it, Luke gives us the detail that Jesus went up a high mountain to pray (Matthew 17:1–13; Mark 9:2–13; Luke 9:28–36). All three gospel writers tell us that Jesus brought three followers with him: Peter, James, and John.

> While Jesus prayed, something remarkable happened.
> He was transfigured. What on earth does it mean to be
> transfigured? We don't exactly know. Jesus' form was
> somehow changed. His clothes were brighter white
> than anything ever seen before, but his actual body was
> somehow different. It was glorified.

According to Mark 9, Jesus and three of his closest followers had just come from a mountaintop experience. Peter, James, and John might have described it as a perfect day. They had been given a glimpse of Jesus in a transfigured, glorious form. They had looked on as Jesus miraculously spoke to two ancient heroes of the faith: Elijah and Moses. Then a cloud had covered them. God had spoken. And they had heard him.

It was so perfect, so glorious, that Peter had wanted to build shelters and extend the visit.

But they had to leave the peak and get back to life at the base of the mountain. They had to withdraw from the heights and re-enter the depths.

Why?

Because God was at work on the ground. God had boots at the bottom. God was a light shining in darkness. He was glory amidst shame.

When Jesus arrived at the bottom, he walked into a mess. A man was desperate to find healing for his son. The situation seemed impossible, but Jesus said to the father, "Everything is possible for one who believes" (verse 23).

Passage Prep for Parents

- Describe a perfect day with your kids. If you've experienced one, what did it look like? If you haven't, what might it look like?

- What were the boy's symptoms (verses 18, 20, 22, 25)?

- What words would you use to describe this father's life as a parent?

- Why does Jesus say the disciples can't heal the boy (verses 19, 29)? What is the connection between these two verses?

- What would a perfect day look like for this father?

- The disciples are surprised by their inability to heal in this situation. Why? (Read Matthew 10:1; Mark 6:6–13; Luke 9:1–6.)

What Went Wrong?

The commotion at the base of the mountain is caused by the disciples' inability to heal a demon-possessed boy. Nine followers of Jesus appear to have no healing power. They can't understand it. It's worked before. In fact, in Mark 6:6–13 we learn that Jesus sent out the twelve "two by two and gave them authority over impure spirits" (verse 7) And they were successful: "They went out and preached that people should repent. They drove out many demons and anointed many sick people with oil and healed them" (verses 12–13).

But now, for some reason, the disciples cannot drive out a demon from a *child*. And everybody is watching. And not everybody in the crowd really wants the disciples to succeed in the first place. Religious leaders—the Bible teachers of the day—opposed Jesus and his followers. So at the first sign of distress, they took the opportunity to pounce on the disciples.

SCRIPTURE INSIGHT

Matthew devoted an entire chapter, forty-two verses, to describing Jesus sending out the twelve. Jesus "gave them authority to drive out impure spirits and to heal every disease and sickness" (10:1). He said: "As you go, proclaim this message: 'The kingdom of heaven has come near.' Heal the sick, raise the dead, cleanse those who have leprosy, drive out demons" (verses 7–8).

Luke also recorded that Jesus "gave them power and authority to drive out all demons and to cure diseases, and he sent them out to proclaim the kingdom of God and to heal the sick" (9:1–2).

Waiting for Failure

Sometimes in life we come across people who find some pleasure in seeing others fail.

I have a friend who cannot succeed as a parent in the eyes of her mother-in-law. In fact, when the kids spend time with Grandma, Grandma actually changes their clothes to more "suitable fashions." She comments on the nap schedule or even the weight that her daughter-in-law has gained. This woman is not a champion of her daughter-in-law; she's a critic.

But I've also seen this tension played out in reverse—when a mother-in-law can't do anything right in the eyes of her daughter-in-law: "You *used* that sippy cup? *Those* baby wipes? He missed his nap while

I was out? What temperature was the bottle? She got a smart phone at *what* age?" Condemnation instead of commendation.

The religious leaders want Jesus' disciples to fail. When it becomes clear that the disciples can't heal the boy, they won't let the disgraced miracle workers slip quietly back into the crowd. They make a spectacle. They want to shame them. So they argue with them right there in front of everyone. The accusations begin flying and soar into a full-blown argument.

Shame on You; Shame on Me

In Bible times, the thrust of an argument wasn't about right and wrong. It was about honor and shame. When we step into this particular argument, we're seeing a battle for honor. The religious leaders want to siphon honor away from Jesus' disciples and, by association, away from Jesus. And they do it *publicly*.

In their book *Misreading Scripture with Western Eyes: Removing Cultural Blinders to Better Understand the Bible*, Randolph Richards and Brandon O'Brien argue that in the Bible and in Eastern cultures, public questions were challenges to honor. They were honor contests. Private questions, on the other hand—like Nicodemus coming at night (John 3:1–21), or the disciples asking Jesus to explain something after the fact (Mark 9:28)—were sincere truth-seeking inquiries.

We're not told that a specific question was raised during the argument, but it's likely that the religious leaders wanted to know *why* the disciples couldn't heal the boy. Is their leader really of *God*? The argument is public. The crowd will decide the verdict. If the crowd agrees with the religious leaders, then Jesus and his followers lose honor, and the religious leaders gain it. If the crowd agrees with the disciples, then the religious leaders lose honor, and Jesus and his followers gain it.

Shamers work to make people believe there's something about them that makes them unworthy of companionship, love, affection, human touch, or trust. Shamers get the community to turn against the individuals they want to shame.

Bowling over Shame

Lice visited my friend's house. She has four kids. Not all of them got it, but she did. My friend said going through the grocery store with a cart filled with lice treatment warded off even the kindest souls. The contents of her cart shamed her. Customers don't strike up a conversation the way they do when they see a birthday cake and candles in your shopping cart: "Looks like you're having a party!" When your cart is loaded with lice liquidator, nobody exclaims, "Looks like you've got lice!" Instead they whisper it inside their own minds and among other shoppers and casually shift away from your line with some half-hearted excuse like, "Oh, I think I forgot the bread." They don't ask you to hold their place in line. And that's fine. You've got bigger fish to fry.

Shamed at the grocery store.

My friend stripped all of the beds. She washed every article of clothing in special detergent—several times over. Got rid of stuffed animals. Sanitized. Several weeks after the plague of lice had ended, her unaffected daughter was invited to a bowling birthday party. The little girl was excited for her first candlepin excursion.

But a few days before the party, my friend got a phone call from the mother of the birthday girl. "Please have your daughter wear her hair in a bun." My friend was surprised but muttered an automatic "Okay" in response. She explained that the pesky critters were indeed gone. In fact, this particular daughter never even had lice. All heads were clean. Daily inspections. No eggs. If there were any hint or suspicion of a problem, my friend wouldn't have accepted the invitation.

The birthday bowling day rolled around. It was clear my friend's daughter already had three strikes against her. When she hopped in the car with the other girls, everyone leaned away from her, like falling candlepins. When they arrived at the bowling alley, the coats were piled on a row of chairs. My friend's daughter watched as her coat was removed from the pile, stuffed under the chairs, on the floor, and kicked into the corner by a size seven-and-a-half salt-stained boot.

Nine years old and shamed at the bowling alley.

I remember changing for gym in the middle school locker room. A band of girls burst into the empty stall next to mine and grabbed the pair of jeans that another girl had left there. They examined the tag. After crumpling the pants back onto the bench, the girls giggled and began their vicious campaign. *Lisa wears size ten.* Shamed in the locker room.

From that point on, I wore my gym clothes to school. I *never* changed in the locker room.

Today, teens are ruthlessly shamed on social media when peers point out physical traits or academic deficits or emotional shortcomings or embarrassing episodes or serious secrets. The goal is to get others to break connection with the victim, thereby shaming that person.

Where Is Jesus?

Unable to heal the demon-possessed boy, the disciples are shamed by the religious leaders. The goal is to discredit them further and get the rest of the crowd to break connection with them. The disciples are in danger of being dishonored.

These men need help. Where is Jesus?

But in the middle of this argument stands a father with his son. The religious leaders don't care about his son. They want to dishonor the disciples. Maybe the disciples have even lost sight of the hurting father and boy. They just want to *do* a miracle.

There's a difference between doing a miracle and caring for a person who needs a miracle. Does anybody actually care about this father and his son and all that they've been through? The shame *they've* experienced as a family raising a demoniac? Nothing severs the community connection like raising a son who is tormented by the devil. Nothing brings more shame on a family than the knowledge that Satan has infiltrated one's home and holds someone hostage.

Let's face it: as parents, we care the most. When it comes to our children, nobody else will ever worry as much as we do, cry as much as we do, strategize as much as we do, do as much as we do, spend as much as we do. Nobody. Parents bear the brunt of agonizing over their kids.

This father bears that burden. Nobody cares about his son more than he does. Organized religion doesn't. Jesus' followers don't. The neighbors don't.

But Jesus does.

Insults fly like burning arrows aimed at piercing the opponent. The father and son are caught in the crossfire of religion gone bad. He covers his son. He is in a crowd of people, yet he is alone. Again.

This man needs help. *Where is Jesus?*

SCRIPTURE INSIGHT

"Jesus Is Messiah"
Many scholars speculate over why it was Elijah and Moses who appeared with Jesus at the transfiguration (Mark 9:2–13). Elijah was an Old Testament prophet

and miracle worker who never tasted death. Instead, God whisked him "up into heaven in a whirlwind" (2 Kings 2:11). Jews still leave a cup of wine at their Seder meal for Elijah in the hope of his visiting their homes and announcing the coming of the Messiah, the long-expected one who would reign and restore the Jewish people. Jews believed that before the Messiah came, the end times would begin with the appearance of Elijah.[9]

Jews also expected that the Messiah would be a prophet like Moses (Deuteronomy 18:15, 18). The appearance of both of these men point to Jesus as the Messiah.

"Jesus Is the Son of God"

A cloud enveloped the mountaintop, and God spoke: "This is my Son, whom I love. Listen to him!" (Mark 9:7) The disciples began to realize that the kingdom Jesus had been talking about was much more involved than they had ever imagined, because the Messiah was none other than the Son of God. Nobody had been expecting that.

What do you say after that? What *can* you say after that? Jesus' glory is undeniable.

"Shame before Glory"

But his shame is undeniable, too. Moses and Elijah also evoke less than glorious images. Both men suffered at the hands of their own people. Both men experienced rejection. Jesus spoke to the three disciples about the suffering and rejection he would be facing. There would be glory. But there would also be shame. Shame before glory. There would be death on a wooden cross. And nothing was more shameful than that.

Comin' Down the Mountain

Jesus and the three disciples were on the descent from glory into the crowd, where the other disciples were losing glory at the hands of the religious establishment.

The transfiguration in the previous section of Mark 9 and the argument in verse 14 are connected. Mark painted a stark contrast: the transfiguration dealt with Jesus' undisputed glory and honor, but the descent to the bottom of the mountain revealed an attempt to strip glory and honor from Jesus and his followers by discrediting them publicly for their inability to heal. It seems ridiculous that the glory that had been revealed on the mountain would have to be defended on the ground. The unbelieving at the base were blind to the honor that had been evident on the peak.

Out of this mountaintop moment, Jesus enters into an argument. The Son of God is in the midst of human sin and suffering.

Read that again. *The Son of God is in the midst of human sin and suffering.* He's God on the ground. God doesn't shy away from our messy lives as we raise our children. He enters into the mess.

And God on the ground is disappointed by what he sees. He asks, "What are you arguing with them about?" (verse 16). The disciples don't answer. Neither do the religious leaders. Instead, the father in the middle speaks up: "Teacher, I brought you my son, who is possessed by a spirit that has robbed him of speech. Whenever it seizes him, it throws him to the ground. He foams at the mouth, gnashes his teeth and becomes rigid. I asked your disciples to drive out the spirit, but they could not" (verses 17–18).

Jesus says: "You unbelieving generation…how long shall I stay with you? How long shall I put up with you? Bring the boy to me" (verse 19).

The argument is over. Jesus has a way of getting to the heart of the matter. At the core of the situation is unbelief.

But who is unbelieving? To whom is Jesus speaking? The disciples? The religious leaders? The father of the boy? Me?

He's talking to everyone.

Unbelieving Followers

The disciples weren't trusting God for the power to heal. They were relying on their own strength. Disconnected from their source of power, they could never perform a miracle. Failing to believe that their power to heal came from Jesus, the disciples were left inept.

But they had believed—in the past. Jesus had sent them out to preach the gospel and heal the sick and demon-possessed (Mark 6:7–13). And they did it with great success. They came back to Jesus and reported all that they had done (Mark 6:30). I can imagine the stories. Twelve grown men, eager to share their testimonies of preaching and healing, maybe even one-upping each other: "Well, that's nothing! You should have seen what *we* ran into!" But also encouraging each other—happy to be doing the work of the kingdom and grateful for the power of the King.

But something changed. They continued to do the work of healing, but they stopped relying on the healer, and they dismissed the seriousness of the situation. How did that happen?

Maybe they got comfortable with the work of ministry. In the beginning, they were nervous and unsure. They knew their every step was dependent on Jesus. But after some success walking on their own, they felt they didn't need him as much.

As Christian parents, we can do the work of parenting, even as we've stopped relying on our heavenly Father. It's not a conscious decision to disconnect from God. It simply happens in the busyness of the routine. Staying connected to God requires intentionality. It requires deliberate steps to maintain the relationship.

Recognizing Unhealthy Territory

The disciples also lost touch with the gravity of the situation, caught up in their own agendas. The problems this father and son had were too big for them. They failed to reach out for the hand of God. Focused on their own honor being at stake, they did not attend to the precious lives right in front of them.

We can also get caught up in other concerns and forget to attend to the troubles unfolding in our children's lives. As they grow, we have unparalleled opportunity to help them navigate the world, to discern the healthy from the unhealthy, and to parse out the many messages they are receiving: in school, in church, at home.

- Are our children learning that they are incredibly loved by God and made in his image?

- What messages do social media give our kids?

- What is a helpful marker in determining when a child can have the world at his or her fingertips in a smartphone?

- What movies and TV shows support the fruit of the spirit—"love, joy, peace, forbearance [patience], kindness, goodness, faithfulness, gentleness and self-control" (Galatians 5:22–23)?

- What media wrestle with good and evil and portray good as an admirable quality?

Do our children experience grace and love at school? Do they give and accept forgiveness on the playground? What do our kids learn by the way we argue at home? I have a friend who says he never remembers his parents ever fighting. When they argued, they went behind closed doors. No raised voices. At the other end of the spectrum are parents who enter into shouting matches while their children become spectators (and perhaps even scorekeepers). Somewhere between the two extremes is a happy medium—a place where parents reveal their differences with respect and dignity.

The disciples missed what was happening. They thought the most important thing at stake was their honor, but it was the people who had come to them for help who mattered more. They needed to reach out for the hand of Jesus. As parents, so do we.

Recognizing God's Power

Or maybe the disciples thought that this little boy's case was indeed impossible. Maybe they thought it was simply too difficult for God.

It's easy to understand why the father begins by saying to Jesus, *"If you can do anything."* He has just witnessed Jesus' followers' *inability* to heal.

Maybe his son's case *is* too complicated for Jesus. It's too entwined in evil for Jesus. It's stronger than Jesus. It's smarter than Jesus. It's more persistent than Jesus.

Parents in this century might easily raise the same doubts. "Is what my child faces too much for God? It might not be possible for him. It's beyond him." We think that way because it's been too much for family or counselors or teachers or ministry leaders.

Doubt is a hard place for parents. Dangling from the back slope of a question mark, we cry: "Are you able?" "How?" "Why?" "What now?" But no parent wants to live life clinging to a question mark of doubt.

The Mixture of Belief and Unbelief

And it's not that we have no faith in God. But that faith is mixed with unbelief. We often live with a mixture of *if it is possible* and *everything is possible*. Just like the rest of us, this father lives with a combination of belief and unbelief.

I have a very vivid childhood memory of one night around the family dinner table. I was about twelve years old, and my uncle was eating at our house. He grabbed the Italian dressing in his right hand. Since the oil and vinegar were separated, he shook it with vigor up over his shoulder to make a homogenous mixture. But the cap was off the bottle, launching oil and vinegar like an erupting volcano. It splattered the refrigerator, floor, and cabinets with a slick Sicilian veneer. My sisters and I burst out laughing.

Like the oil and vinegar mixture of the dressing, there is a mixture of belief and unbelief in all of us. That contrast comes pouring out when we are shaken.

Kids are great at shaking up their parents. That's when mothers and fathers realize unbelief is mixed with their belief. Lack of trust is mixed with trust.

But even so, God still responds to a parent's mixture of faith and faithlessness.

Parents might believe that Jesus died for their sin and was resurrected on the third day, but when they ask God to provide for their child's academic deficit, they say, "If it is possible." Parents trust that they have been forgiven by a holy and righteous God, but when they ask God for wisdom regarding their child's behavioral issues, they mutter, "If it is possible." We trust that we have eternal life, but when we ask God for comfort in this life, we rattle off the refrain, "If it is possible."

Parents Can Spread Hope to Other Parents

Yes, this father trusts that Jesus can heal his son, but there's still a piece of him that *doesn't*. The piece that doesn't believe is based on what the father has seen and what he's experienced. The father knows that his son is severely affected. This isn't a passing state of being. It's everyday life. He's seen the damage caused to his son and his whole family. The father tells Jesus that the demon often tries to *burn his son or drown him*. An assassin has taken up residence inside his son's body. The father has experienced the shame of the community. He also knows that Jesus' closest followers are not able to help.

When the father asks Jesus to help him overcome his unbelief, Jesus answers that cry for help with swift deliverance. He demonstrates his power and heals the boy. That's what this father needed to overcome his unbelief.

God has conquered sin and raised Jesus from the dead. He can handle our kids. Parents don't need to ask *if you can, if it's possible—but there's grace even when we do.* Everything is possible for one who believes.

SCRIPTURE INSIGHT

"Shame on Him"

Jesus spoke words similar to the father's words when he said "If it is possible" to his Father (Matthew 26:39). He prayed the words in a garden. At night. Sweat like blood fell to the ground as he agonized over his impending death (Luke 22:44). Yes, death frightened him. But it was more than death. It was separation from his heavenly Father—something he'd never, ever experienced. It was carrying the weight of every human sin on his sinless shoulders. On his sinless soul. He had never experienced the burden of sin. Now every sin ever committed—past, present, future—was his burden. He owned it. He would suffer for it.

It comforts me to know that in Jesus' most heart-wrenching moment, he cried out to God words similar to those that a hurting father cried out to him: "If it is possible"—"If you can do anything."

But when Jesus prayed to his loving Father "If it is possible," he was not doubting his heavenly Father. There was no mixture of belief and unbelief. Jesus was not questioning God by asking "Are you able?" He was asking "Are you willing?"

This garden moment reminds parents that God is *able* to walk us through the most challenging circumstances with our children. But this garden moment does something even more powerful. It's depicts something *honest*. It's an honest look at fear and sadness—emotions that every parent experiences with their children. It doesn't soften the hard reality that difficult times with our kids are filled with tears, yearnings, exhaustion, pleading, and deep, deep heartache. God doesn't tell Jesus to quit crying or to show a stiff upper lip. God allows Jesus…*he allows himself*…to be overwhelmed in sorrow. God is in the garden with parents, and he will help us handle his will.

"He was pierced for our transgressions, he was crushed for our iniquities; the punishment that brought us peace was upon him, and by his wounds we are healed…. After he has suffered, he will see the light of life and be satisfied." (Isaiah 53:5, 11)

"Glory to Him"

The Gospels report that three days after Jesus was crucified, God resurrected Jesus. Jesus knew that God was able to raise him from the dead. He even spoke about it to his disciples. After he freed the boy from the demon, Jesus spent time teaching his disciples in private. He said: "The Son of Man is going to be delivered into the hands of men. They will kill him, and after three days he will rise" (Mark 9:31).

Even when parents doubt, Jesus' unwavering faith provides a solid foundation for us. We can stand on it when our faith falters. Jesus did not go to the cross unsure if God had the power to accomplish his resurrection. Jesus did not go to the cross uncertain of God's ability to raise him from the dead. He never asked, "If it is possible, if you are able, raise me from the dead." Jesus knew all things were possible with God, yet removing the cup of suffering was not part of God's will. God was putting into motion an epic plan of salvation.

Sometimes God's will seems so harsh. But God's good purposes are always at the center of his perfect will. His will brings peace and healing. The shame of the cross was endured first. Glory followed.

Big Hero God

It was Holy Week when my friend's five-year old daughter, Ellie, was diagnosed with cancer. Neuroblastoma is a serious cancer. Stage 4 is even worse, because the cancer has been copied four times. Radiation, chemotherapy, and immunotherapy treatments began immediately.

Kate and Andy have two younger children to care for as well. They spent months at Boston Children's Hospital, where Ellie battled fevers and infections, liver disease as a result of medication, recovering from surgery, and managing food intake. When at home, Ellie spends her days in a special bedroom and bathroom built by loving church members. Her mattress is medical grade—made especially for kids with cancer. Her bathroom is for her use alone and nobody else's. She uses it frequently throughout the day and long nights, when diarrhea keeps her and her parents awake. She's had many emergency trips back into Boston because of fevers and persistent nosebleeds. She has lost a good deal of her ability to hear. Every nerve-wracking stint in the hospital is followed by a rocky re-entry into the routine of family life among younger siblings. Ellie's outcome is uncertain.

The team at Children's never gives parents the whole picture. They give it one stage at a time. They explain what one might expect during a particular phase. That's it. Each phase of treatment has challenges of its own. Ellie's mom said that when they've wondered how they'd make it through the next phase, God shows up in a bigger way than before. Yes, of course, these parents have good days and bad days. They endure hours of complete frustration and hours of tears. They have moments of unparalleled faith and days of dark doubt. But in every instance, God has never been too small. He's bigger. Then even bigger. And bigger still. Kate and Andy believe that God is bigger than anything they'll face. Most days, "if it is possible" is not part of their vocabulary. But when it is, God's grace is big enough for them.

Now that official treatment has ended, it's a game of wait and see. The ultimate prognosis was described as a "coin toss." That's a fatalistic phrase. It's not a phrase of faith. No matter how we feel, in the darkest moments of parenting, it's never a coin toss. It's always in God's loving, perfect hands.

When I sat with Ellie's mom during Holy Week, a year after the diagnosis, she was filled with hope. Hope floods her soul because she believes that Easter was God's gracious timing to reveal Ellie's disease. The hope of Easter resurrection is real to them, because God is bigger than death. Everything is possible with God.

Ellie's mom and dad know that from a human perspective, the medical outcome is uncertain. But they see life from a faith perspective. They know God is able to heal. They also know that God is no stranger to the thorny garden. He is with them as they cry and yearn and plead and suffer sorrow upon sorrow. Even more, they know that God can raise the dead. They trust that God will be bigger for whatever comes next. And in the end, glory comes to every believer in Jesus Christ, because Jesus took our shame.

SUMMARY

- God is concerned about parents.
- Shamers work to get people to break connection with an individual.
- The New Testament was written in an honor-shame culture.
- On the cross, Jesus took our shame; in exchange, we got his glory.
- Most people harbor a mixture of belief and unbelief.
- Parents must rely on God's strength.
- Parents must lovingly guide their children.
- Everything is possible with God.

READ

Mark 9:2–13

Isaiah 53

TAKE ACTION

Write down a couple of areas in life that might be detrimental for your kids (social media, trends in clothing, TV programs, video games, and so on). What steps might you take to safeguard your children in these particular areas?

PRAY

Dear God of Glory,

I pray for moms and dads who feel shame. I pray that they would know your forgiveness.

I pray for those who are being shamed. Especially young people. Give them strength to endure. Protect them. Help me to recognize when my children might need my guiding hand. Show me how to respond.

Circumstances in my life have shaken me, and I've discovered that unbelief exists alongside my belief. Help me with my unbelief.

I pray for parents who care for very sick children. Increase their faith. Increase their stamina. Increase their wisdom and their joy.

I pray for their children. Increase their faith, too. You said, "Let the little children come." I pray the most vulnerable among us would be fortified by your strength.

I pray for _____, a small child with a big sickness. I pray for your healing hand.

I'm grateful that you have planned a day when all disease and sickness, all hurt and pain, all sadness and sorrow will be gone forever. You are a big, glorious God.

Amen.

Questions for Personal Reflection or Group Discussion

1. Has anyone ever tried to shame you? Briefly describe the situation.

2. What situation with your child seems impossible right now?

3. What has shaken you as a parent and revealed the mixture of belief and unbelief coexisting in your heart and mind?

4. How do you stay connected to God?

5. Identify seasons or times in which you have relied more or less on God.

CHAPTER 4

Faith to the Finish Line

John 4:43–54

After the two days he left for Galilee. (Now Jesus himself had pointed out that a prophet has no honor in his own country.) When he arrived in Galilee, the Galileans welcomed him. They had seen all that he had done in Jerusalem at the Passover Festival, for they also had been there.

Once more he visited Cana in Galilee, where he had turned the water into wine. And there was a certain royal official whose son lay sick at Capernaum. When this man heard that Jesus had arrived in Galilee from Judea, he went to him and begged him to come and heal his son, who was close to death.

"Unless you people see signs and wonders," Jesus told him, "you will never believe."

The royal official said, "Sir, come down before my child dies."

"Go," Jesus replied, "your son will live."

The man took Jesus at his word and departed. While he was still on the way, his servants met him with the news that his boy was living. When he inquired as to the time when his son got better, they said to him, "Yesterday, at one in the afternoon, the fever left him."

Then the father realized that this was the exact time at which Jesus had said to him, "Your son will live." So he and his whole household believed.

This was the second sign Jesus performed after coming from Judea to Galilee.

What Jesus said to parents:
Unless you people see signs and wonders…you will never believe.

The Parenting Marathon

It's a raw, blustery April day as I write this chapter. The thermometer reads 38 degrees. The cat is curled up against the gas fireplace. The dogs find warmth in the nest of my lap. It's Patriots' Day and also the start of school vacation. My oldest is disappointed because the library is closed. His little brothers are two miles down the road at an indoor rock-climbing facility. Those rocks will get a workout. It's Monday. Marathon Monday.

The Boston Marathon is the oldest running marathon in the world, dating back to 1897. The inspiration for the Boston Marathon was the revived 1896 Olympics in Athens, in which the very first modern marathon took place. Such races are named for the battle of Marathon in 490 BC. One legend has it that the soldier Pheidippides ran from Marathon to Athens in order to deliver the good news that the Greeks had defeated the Persians. He yelled, "Niki! Niki!" which translated from the Greek means "victory" (and yes, the sneaker company Nike finds its roots in that word). The journey was somewhere between twenty-four and twenty-six miles long. Soon after he delivered the news, he collapsed and died.

Parenting feels like a marathon, with a suppertime sprint every afternoon. (Dishing out dinner is my daily heartbreak hill.) When we finally get the kids down and reach the bedtime finish line, we shout

"Niki!" only to collapse under the weight of laundry and lunches and loading the dishwasher. Parenting hasn't killed us, but we've sustained some battle scars.

Every parent bears the battle bruises of raising children. Maybe they've come from the bedtime battle, the burping at the table battle, or the talking-back battle. What mother or father hasn't run the race for respect, engaged in the culture conflict, or experienced a technology tiff or the homework wars or the friends' face-off? Parents often wonder what victory in these skirmishes even looks like.

Sometimes parents fight *with* their children. Other times the battle is *for* their children—for the academic support that's needed, for the medical care that's needed, for emotional well-being, for spiritual maturity. Is there a clear finish line to cross? Or is it a race that never ends?

The father described in John 4:43–54 charges uphill for more than twenty miles. He races for victory, but he's not racing for himself. Like a modern marathon runner with Miles for Miracles,[10] his patient-partner is his dying son. The route runs west-southwest from the starting line in the seaside town of Capernaum. Somewhere along the elevated reed-swept plains of Cana, he will cross the finish line at the feet of Jesus. It is a race this father must run. His son's life depends on it. But Jesus doesn't greet him the way he expected. No crown of victory. No pat on the back. No offer of water from the well. No encouraging words. Instead, Jesus says, "Unless you people see signs and wonders…you will never believe!"

Passage Prep for Parents

- How might you reconcile verse 44 ("Now Jesus himself had pointed out that a prophet has no honor in his own country") with verse 45 ("When he arrived in Galilee, the Galileans welcomed him")?

- The royal official worked for Herod. We don't know if he was Greek or Jewish. How might the crowd respond to the official if he were Greek? Would their response be different if he were Jewish?

- In his gospel, John uses the word *signs* instead of *miracles*. Why do you think John uses the word *signs*?

- John supplies a definition of *faith* in verse 50: "The man took Jesus at his word." Explain that sentence in your own words.

Bringing Our *One Thing* to Jesus

The royal official could have sent a servant to Jesus. *Ordered* someone else to go. But his son's life hangs in the balance. It's a race that only a parent can run. He pecks his wife on the cheek goodbye. A sea breeze glides off of Galilee, leaving ripples of waves in its wake before it fills the room where the boy lies sleeping. His son is too weak to wish him farewell. He swishes away the hair from the boy's forehead and wipes the sweat of fever off his brow.

The man is identified as a "royal official" (verse 46). But at home, he's known as *Pater*, "Father." He works for Herod Antipas but lives in the fishing village of Capernaum along the northwest coast of the Sea of Galilee. Herod's palace was located in the city of Tiberias, along the southwest coast of the sea, about ten miles from Capernaum. That was likely close enough. The official could maintain the perks and benefits of a royal connection without dealing with the daily drama of palace life. And there was plenty of drama. Herod Antipas, who ruled the region of Galilee in Northern Israel, created an uproar when he married his half-brother's wife, Herodias. One prophet, John the Baptist, was particularly upset about this breach of ethics …and he made his opinion known. It cost him his head. *On a platter.*

At Herod's own birthday celebration. Distance, the royal official might have determined, does indeed make the heart grow fonder. Or at least keeps it beating.

The royal official has everything he needs in Capernaum:

- A paycheck from Herod
- Invitations to hobnob at fancy events
- Connections to the wealthy and powerful
- A home by the sea
- Servants and a family
- Distance from the domestic difficulties of Herod's household

But there is *one thing* his money and connections can't buy: his son's healing.

So this desperate parent brings this *one thing* to Jesus. But when he does, Jesus responds with a reprimand.

My heart sinks when I read the reprimand. Why? Because this father is *fragile,* and I want Jesus to be gentle with me when I bring my *one thing* to him. Why on earth is he stern with this father?

Because this approach will set the stage to give the father a more significant victory than he ever imagined. *Much more.*

He Saw the Signs

It's likely the official had seen Jesus in and around Capernaum. After all, Capernaum was Jesus' home base for ministry.[11] He called five of his disciples from Capernaum: Peter, Andrew, James, John, and Matthew. It was a city in which Jews and Gentiles (non-Jews) lived side by side. It bustled with commercial activity: fishing and trade. It also bustled with the Roman occupiers. A garrison of about a hundred soldiers was stationed in Capernaum, and the Roman official even lived in the city (Matthew 8:5–13). Situated along the road that led to Damascus, Capernaum was home to a Roman toll station.[12] Cross the border and pay your toll. Perhaps Jesus' disciple Matthew collected the tax in this border tollbooth.

Over time, Jesus performed many miracles in Capernaum that surely would have caught the attention of the official. Not all of the miracles occurred prior the official's request in this passage by John; but nevertheless, Jesus had an active ministry of miracles and wonder-working in Capernaum.[13] The official would have been familiar with Jesus.

- Five thousand people who have just been miraculously fed don't slip quietly away from the countryside without spreading news of the miracle (John 6:1–15).

- The miraculous catch of fish might have made the *Jerusalem Times* or at least the *Fisherman's Quarterly,* and it might have given the industry a public relations boost (John 21:4–14).

- The healing of the demon-possessed man on the Sabbath in the synagogue was witnessed by many worshipers (Mark 1:21–28).

- Surely Peter's mother-in-law told the neighbors that Jesus freed her from the fever (Matthew 8:14–15).

- The bold rooftop offensive of the paralytic's friends must have been the talk around the well for weeks (Matthew 9:2–8; Mark 2:1–12; Luke 5:17–20).

- Jesus healed the woman with the issue of blood in the midst of a crushing crowd (Mark 5:25–34).

But perhaps the miracle that most touched the official was the healing of Jairus's daughter (Matthew 9:18–26; Mark 5:21–43; Luke 8:41–56). Another father—and one in the same community—understood what it was like to watch a child fade away. Another father—in the same town—understood what it meant to seek Jesus with a desperate plea for help.

Genuine Faith

But even with so many miracles, people in Capernaum didn't have *true* faith in Jesus. Yes, people believed he existed. They believed he could do miracles. But they had trouble believing that he was the Messiah and that he was the Son of God, the Giver of life.

John's gospel is all about *genuine* faith in Jesus. In fact, a key verse in the book of John that describes the purpose of his writing is found in chapter 20:30–31: "Jesus performed many other signs in the presence of his disciples, which are not recorded in this book. But these are written that you may believe that Jesus is the Messiah, the Son of God, and that by believing you may have life in his name."

Genuine faith, according to the gospel writer, included three beliefs:

- Jesus is the Messiah.
- Jesus is the Son of God.
- Trusting in Jesus results in life.

What kind of faith did this father who worked for Herod have? Was it genuine? Or was it more superficial?

God's Plan for Parents

This father has no idea that the journey he has embarked upon is not only for his son but is also for *him*. Jesus' primary work will be with the faith of the father. Sometimes God's greater work is with mothers and fathers. As they pray for God to move in the lives of their children, God moves in their own lives and gives them the opportunity to demonstrate genuine faith.

Leaving the sea behind him, this dad dashes across the landscape, racing for his son's life. He does not yet know that God has a plan for his entire family. He races with one goal in mind. But God has many. God has more in store for this father than he could ever imagine.

Traveling from Capernaum to Cana could have taken about a day (today, driving between the two cities would take about an hour). The father likely broke up this hike of over twenty miles by sheltering at an inn overnight somewhere between the two towns. He reaches Jesus in Cana around 1:00 in the afternoon.

When the father approaches Jesus and asks him to leave Cana to come to Capernaum to heal his son, Jesus responds to everyone present with a startling rebuke: "Unless you people see signs and wonders…you will never believe" (verse 48).

Sign Stop

In his gospel, John refers to miracles as *signs*. People wanted to see signs from Jesus to prove that he really was something special. But they could never get beyond the signs. They didn't understand that the miraculous signs pointed to something greater—insight into who Jesus was.

Imagine a woman in labor, and her husband rushing her to the hospital. All along the route she periodically sees a blue sign with a white capital *H* on it. It's the sign that directs the driver toward the hospital. It's the sign that indicates the hospital is nearby. But imagine that her husband pulls over onto the side of the road and parks the car underneath the H sign and announces with joy, "Honey, we're here!" Meanwhile, traffic whizzes by as her contractions gain traction.

Of course, it would be ridiculous to stop at the H sign. The goal is the hospital. The sign only points to the destination. But in Jesus' day— as in our own—people gathered around the sign. They couldn't get beyond the sign. They couldn't see that the sign pointed to something far greater—the truth about who Jesus was:

- Messiah
- Son of God
- Giver of life

But in this particular case, on this particular day, the people demand a sign for another reason. They want proof that this father, an employee of Herod's, is worthy of Jesus' time and attention. The official in our passage is on Herod's payroll. That makes him disliked by everyday Jews. We don't know if this father is a Gentile or a Jew. Either way, the Jews don't care for him. If he's a Gentile, he has that against him, in addition to working for Herod. If he's a Jew, then he has sold out by working for Herod. Herod is in league with Rome, and Rome is the enemy.

The Galileans can't understand why Jesus would even consider healing this man's son. He doesn't deserve it, but they need to see it. They need a sign. They need to see that Jesus' love extends to the man they despise. They can't simply believe that Jesus would love such a person.

But he does. Jesus loves this father. Jesus loves the outsider.

Jesus Loves the Outsider

In the passage that precedes this one in John, Jesus spends time in the despised land of Samaria (4:4–6). Even more, Jesus spends time talking to a woman of ill repute under the noontime sun at the village well (4:7–26). His heart for outsiders beats stronger than the drum of conventional wisdom.

This female Samaritan outsider tells the village about Jesus (4:28–30). Her testimony is received with interest and enthusiasm, and the Samaritans urge Jesus to stay for a few days in order to teach them (4:39–42). He performs no miracles. He gives them no signs. *Yet the Samaritans believe in Jesus.* These presumed outsiders put their trust in Jesus solely based on what he says, while the insiders do not have faith, even though they've seen signs and wonders.

Will the father in this passage have faith like the Samaritans, or will he demand a sign like the Jews? It's a question all parents must ask when running to Jesus on behalf of their children. Are we trusting Jesus' word, or are we making demands of him?

The father doesn't flinch after Jesus flings his blistering comment about unbelief. Instead, he says to Jesus, "Sir, come down before my child dies" (verse 49). This father trusts that Jesus doesn't see him the way so many of his neighbors do. He believes that Jesus can love him and can heal his son.

Jesus responds, "Go…your son will live" (verse 50).

But will this parent take Jesus at his word? Will he trust that when Jesus says "your son will live," he means it? Can this father turn around and walk back home, or will he demand more from Jesus? This is the bare essence of faith—taking Jesus at his word.

Parenting by faith means taking Jesus at his word. It's trusting him with our kids. It's laying our kids at his feet and being able to walk away, knowing that our sons and daughters are in the hands of God. God doesn't need to prove anything to us. We need no signs. We don't need to make demands of God or set conditions. His word is enough.

Honoring Jesus

And that's the difference between honoring Jesus and welcoming him. We honor Jesus when we trust his word. John tells us that "Jesus himself had pointed out that a prophet has no honor in his own country" (verse 44). But in the very next verse, John writes that Jesus was welcomed by the people of Galilee: "When he arrived in Galilee, the Galileans welcomed him. They had seen all that he had done in Jerusalem at the Passover Festival, for they also had been there." So which is it? Did Jesus have no honor there, or was he welcomed? The Galileans only welcomed Jesus for his miracles and signs. They didn't honor him. They didn't move beyond the sign to see who Jesus really was. They didn't trust his word.

But this father does.

Jesus says to him: "Go…your son will live." A better but more cryptic translation is "Go…your son lives." The phrase "your son lives" is a bit ambiguous. The boy was living when the father left him a day earlier, but he was also dying. It's a confusing statement. Jesus doesn't spell it out. Is the boy going to continue living, or is Jesus simply stating a fact that presently the son lives?

In ancient times, healings were associated with the healer. They didn't happen apart from the touch of the healer. This father really needs to trust, because Jesus isn't coming with him to Capernaum.

> "Therefore, since we are surrounded by such a great cloud of witnesses, let us throw off everything that hinders and the sin that so easily entangles. And let us run with perseverance the race marked out for us, fixing our eyes on Jesus, the pioneer and perfecter of faith.…Consider him who endured such opposition from sinners, so that you will not grow weary and lose heart." (Hebrews 12:1-3)

He must take Jesus at his word. *Like the Samaritans.* This father is being tested, and he passes the test because he believes Jesus' word *without seeing the sign.*

He turns around and walks the twenty miles or so back to Capernaum. The sound of the brush of reeds fades behind him. This time, the walk is downhill. His feet move more easily, but that doesn't mean his faith does. He likely spends the night at an inn again and resumes his journey at the break of dawn. He's anxious to get home. But before he arrives, his servants meet him with the news that his boy lives. He's no longer dying. His fever left him at 1:00 the previous afternoon.

The official's whole household believes. His wife believes. Any other children he has believe. His servants believe.

But what exactly does his whole household believe? We know they believe that Jesus had the ability to heal, because the royal official went to him in the first place in an act of faith. But the official's faith has been deepened by the healing. He now trusts Jesus' word. He believes that Jesus is who he says he is: Messiah, Son of God, Giver of life.

The official had raced to Jesus for his son's life. What he hadn't expected was that he, along with his whole family, would also receive life. Jesus gave him far more than he had asked for and more than he could have ever imagined. Just like the official, our job is to continue running the course set before us, keeping focused on Jesus. When we do that, our faith will be deepened.

Running Our Course in All Weather

Desiree Linden was the first American woman to win the Boston Marathon in more than three decades. Battling 38-degree temperatures, downpours, and whipping wind, Linden finished in 2:39.54. But halfway through the race, she almost quit. She seriously contemplated leaving the race. In her last mile, the rain beat Boylston Street harder than it had all afternoon.

Parenting is a marathon. Parents run to Jesus for their kids when the kids are not able to. They run on their behalf, like Parent Partners. Kids need moms and dads to go to Jesus for them, sometimes slogging it out in the worst of conditions.

Parenting by faith means that even when we're weary, we keep going to Jesus with our concerns for our kids (or maybe grandkids). We trust him. Then we turn around and go home, believing that God has us and our children and our whole family in his gracious grip. Jesus said "Go" (John 4:50). We go in faith and see what Jesus will do. After all, believing is seeing.

Parents honor Jesus when they take him at his word and stop making demands of the God of the universe. Sometimes it's hard to let God be God. But he knows what he's doing. Parents can trust him with their children.

SUMMARY

- The signs in John's gospel point to three things: Jesus is Messiah, Jesus is the Son of God, and Jesus is the Giver of life.

- The Jewish insiders stopped short at the sign and didn't look beyond it to the truth about Jesus.

- Samaritan outsiders and the royal official took Jesus at his word and had genuine faith.

- Parents must take Jesus at his word without making demands on him.

READ

John 4:1–42

TAKE ACTION

Read John 20:30–31. Explain in writing the three core beliefs of faith.

Thank God for the race he has given you to run.

PRAY

Dear God,

I pray for moms and dads who feel shame. I pray that they would know your forgiveness.

I want to go in faith, but sometimes I stumble. I admit I don't always trust you. Maybe it's because I can't see you. But when my eyes are open to you, evidence of your glory and your love is all around me. Help me to see it.

I bring you my one thing. You know how much I desire it. I trust you with it. If my one thing is a test that serves to strengthen my faith, then give me the patience and love to endure. If my one thing is not within your will, then give me the grace to continue the race with joy and gratitude. I want my faith to be deepened by my experiences, not crushed by them.

I pray that my household would have faith in you. Yes, even the most unlikely members.

Give me the stamina to continue looking toward you in the race you have given me. It has been exhausting, and there are days that I would like to pull over and quit—maybe even run the other way. Keep my eyes focused on you, grateful for your partnership in my marathon.

When my race is easy, may I be helpful to others. When mine is uphill, please send me support.

I pray for _____, who is struggling to continue. Give this parent renewed life and your perspective.

Amen.

Questions for Personal Reflection or Group Discussion

1. Describe a time when you had to fight for your child.

2. What is your *one thing*?

3. Are there any examples in which you think God has been stern with you in order to test your faith? Briefly describe an example.

4. In what specific way do you have to take Jesus at his word when it comes to parenting?

CHAPTER 5

Parenting without Tears

Luke 7:11–17

Soon afterward, Jesus went to a town called Nain, and his disciples and a large crowd went along with him. As he approached the town gate, a dead person was being carried out—the only son of his mother, and she was a widow. And a large crowd from the town was with her. When the Lord saw her, his heart went out to her and he said, "Don't cry."

Then he went up and touched the bier they were carrying him on, and the bearers stood still. He said, "Young man, I say to you, get up!" The dead man sat up and began to talk, and Jesus gave him back to his mother.

They were all filled with awe and praised God. "A great prophet has appeared among us," they said. "God has come to help his people." This news about Jesus spread throughout Judea and the surrounding country.

What Jesus said to parents:
Don't cry.

No Need to Cry

We never learn the widow's name. She is identified only by her loss: a mother without a son; a woman without a husband. What she lacks serves as a far better descriptor for her than what she has. She is the widow of Nain, but now she is also…what's the word for a parent who has lost a child?

In the United States, we call families who have lost a son or daughter in war Gold Star Families. But there is no word to describe a mother or a father who has lost a child. It's indescribable: "A wife who loses a husband is called a widow. A husband who loses a wife is called a widower. A child who loses his parents is called an orphan. There is no word for a parent who loses a child. That's how awful the loss is."[14]

In Luke 7:11–17, we learn that Jesus has something to say to the parent whose situation is indescribable. His two words may shock, offend, confuse, or comfort. He says to the widow of Nain (actually, it's a *command*), "Don't cry." It seems a foolish or even heartless thing to say at a funeral.

My middle son is our loud crier. When he gets hurt, *everyone* knows it. Whether it's a bee sting, a splinter, or a scraped knee, it's hard to calm him down. We recently kayaked on Lake Winnipesaukee in New Hampshire. This was Sam's first adventure in his own boat. Toward the end of our brief excursion, his kayak got tangled in the waterline floats that mark off the swimming area. First came the tears; then came the sound. An ear-piercing sob. A howling, yowling kind of cry. Rich and I paddled over to where his boat was caught like a fish in a net. We knew what he needed to do, but he couldn't hear us over his wailing. I raised my voice: "Stop crying!" I wasn't angry, but I needed to get through to him. If he wanted to be freed from his entanglement, then he needed to be quiet and listen. This is called a prohibitive command. I commanded him *not* to do something.

In Luke 7:13, the verb *klaiō* ("to cry") is used in a prohibitive command. Jesus commands the widow not to cry. This doesn't mean he yells at her with harshness. We know that his "heart went out to her," so it makes sense that he speaks to her out of compassion. But she's got to stop crying in order to experience a work of God right in her midst. The widow of Nain isn't whimpering softly. This cry is at full-throated throttle.

Jesus uses a present tense verb when he commands the woman not to cry, which often implies an ongoing action. It's as if he's saying, "There's no need to cry like this ever again."

Cry like what?

As if there's no hope. As if Jesus' reach does not extend to the grave.

Passage Prep for Parents

- Do you know what it's like to be identified by something tragic in your life? What happened?

- Can you think of a time when you had to get through to a crying child? What happened? How did you handle it?

- "Don't cry" are the only words that Jesus says to the widow. Do those words surprise you, anger you, or comfort you? What's your reaction and why do you feel this way?

Junior

I met Junior in the spring of 2001 when I pastored a little Baptist church in southern Maine. I was twenty-seven years old. There was a lot I didn't know about being a minister then. I definitely didn't know how to mow the church lawn. We had a beat-up mower in the basement, underneath the baptistery. It spit and spewed and smoked when my husband pulled the cord. One day, Rich was lugging that piece of junk up those rickety steps when a truck rumbled down the drive and parked next door at the Historical Society Building. It was a 1983 blue and white F150 with the word SCROOGE engraved above the front bumper. I took a deep breath and thought, "Our church neighbor is named Scrooge. We're in trouble." I said a quick prayer.

Then Junior, wearing jeans and red suspenders, stepped out of the truck. And there wasn't an ounce of bah-humbug in him. He was the most generous Scrooge I have ever known. It wasn't long before Junior was mowing the church lawn. I remember the conversations we had about the moss on the walkway and how he scraped it, so the elderly and disabled wouldn't slip. He repaired our chapel sign. I never asked him to do any of it. When I said thank you, this man of few words only grinned and gave me his trademark thumbs-up.

When Junior died, I was privileged to take part in his funeral. I recall very little of the funeral service itself, but I'll never forget the ride to the cemetery. Junior's casket wasn't sitting in a hearse. It was placed on the bed of his 1983 blue and white F150 Scrooge truck! His wife sat shotgun while his son drove. Please, feel free to smile. It was funny; it was odd—it was absolutely beautiful.

This funeral procession meandered through meagerly snow-plowed country roads on a well-planned, intentional route that passed all of the places that were special to Junior: his home, his church (the funeral was held in a different venue due to the large crowd), the lodge where he hung out, and, of course, the fire station where he volunteered.

As the procession rolled through town, scores of people from all walks of life—young and old, red and blue, the wealthy and the just-making-ends-meet kind of people—lined the streets. Wedged between snowbanks on a frigid winter's day, they paid tribute to the man they had known and loved. A fire truck, its ladder fully extended, parked in front of the District 1 station and proudly displayed the American flag.

Upon reaching the cemetery, a crowd huddled close to the grave and drew comfort from Scripture and warmth from each other. Then the crowd dispersed and reunited for a luncheon—chili and beans.

The citizens of this small community were not only honoring Junior, but they were also supporting his wife, Sally. An ordinary guy, and the town came out in full force to mourn with the family. The show of support was incredibly moving.

In Romans 12:15, the apostle Paul wrote: "Rejoice with those who rejoice; mourn with those who mourn." This small town knew just how to do that.

Mourn with Those Who Mourn

When I read the story in Luke 7:11–17, I picture a village mourning together. A young man has just died—the only son of his widowed mother. If the death were unexpected and not the result of illness or disease, then there was little time to comprehend the truth of what had happened before the body was committed to the grave. We don't know if this young man had been sick or involved in some kind of accident. Whatever the case, his life had been cut drastically short.

When I pastored my little church in Maine, I had a favorite parishioner (yes, I had favorites), Mac, who enjoyed rides around the countryside and by the ocean. Once a week, he ventured to the cemetery. He drove by his family plot where his wife was buried. His plot was reserved right next to hers with a headstone that indicated his date of birth: September 15, 1925. The date of death was left blank. He told me he liked to "check on things." I always chuckled to myself because I wondered what kind of action he expected to find at a cemetery. But on two occasions, Mac discovered that his very own grave had been accidentally dug! "Checking on things" at the cemetery didn't sound like such a crazy idea after that. Burial preparations, in Mac's case, preceded death!

In New Testament times, a tomb would be monitored for about three days to make sure death was certain. Mistakes could happen, especially in an arid climate when burial was quick (often on the same day of death). But there was no mistake in Luke 7. The Bible tells us that the young man was dead.

Women played the role of mortician. They were responsible for preparing the body by washing it, cutting the nails and hair, and wrapping the body in linen. *Yes, the widow of Nain prepared her own son's body for burial.* Hands and feet were bound with linen, and the face of the deceased was covered with a linen cloth. But this was not done in quiet solitude. As the process took place, family members, neighbors, even professional mourners sung songs of lament and read Scripture. The widow of Nain would have torn her garment several inches from the neckline down as a symbol of how her heart had been torn inside. Tearing, searing pain. That's what she felt.

Then the body would be carried on a bier outside of the village. With the exception of the king, Jews were not buried within city or village walls. The deceased was placed in a sepulcher, a family tomb in a cave. The body was laid on a shelf-like niche inside the cave.

A stone slab covered the entrance of the tomb, preventing wild beasts from entering. After about a year, when the body had decomposed, the bones were collected and placed in a stone box called an ossuary.

For the first week after the burial, the widow would sit quietly, reflectively, in her home. She would sit barefoot. On the floor. No cooking. No bathing.[15]

SCRIPTURE INSIGHT

Upon Jesus' death, the curtain in the temple was torn in two, symbolizing that the barrier between people and

God had been destroyed. But perhaps the tearing of the curtain tells us even more about God, the loving Father: his heart was torn like a garment at the sacrificial death of his only son.[16]

The widow of Nain has done this before. For her husband. Maybe her father. Now for her only child.

But she is not alone. The village streams in and mourns with her. Long before the apostle Paul ever penned those words about mourning to the church at Rome, the people of Nain "mourned with those who mourn."

By the time we meet the widow in Luke 7, she has torn her garment, listened to songs of lament, been comforted by Scripture, and been inundated with visitors. She has trimmed her son's fingernails and toenails as she did when he was a toddler. She has washed his body, as she did when he was an infant. She has cut his hair and was reminded of how he flinched and squirmed as a small boy when the stroke of the blade clipped his dark locks. I wonder how she is even standing and how she has the strength to carry herself to the tomb. Part of the answer lies in the fact that she is not alone. The village mourns with her.

Parents who deal with tragic circumstances have also wondered how they are still standing. They wonder how they will be able to carry on.

And that's exactly when Jesus comes.

A Clash of Emotions

Imagine the scene at the village gate. One crowd is leaving in sadness, while another crowd is coming in gladness. The crowd following Jesus has witnessed him heal the sick, teach like they've never heard before, and cast out demons. This crowd is bubbling with excitement at the anticipation of what Jesus might say or do next. They are the *rejoicers.*

But the village crowd is mourning. They can be heard throughout the town and beyond. It's the sound of grief. Sobbing. Chests heaving. Heads hung low. They are the *mourners.*

It's a clash of emotions between the mourners and the rejoicers. What happens when extreme sadness bumps into joyful gladness?

Mourners feel the sadness even deeper than before.

Clash in the Waiting Room

I have three little boys. I've also had three miscarriages. After each loss, I dreaded going back to the obstetrician. It wasn't the exam that worried me. It was the waiting room. A waiting room filled with pregnant women, bellies bulging with baby-life, while I was dealing with death.

I felt enormous sadness while the women surrounding me felt immense joy. It was a clash of emotions. And somehow, their joy increased my sorrow.

Sometimes it's hard to be sensitive to someone else's sadness. Maybe we don't have the time or the energy, or maybe the system (like the waiting room) isn't set up for "sorrow sensitivity." But Jesus always sets the right tone and responds in the way that best glorifies his heavenly Father. What happens when sorrow collides with the Savior? Something totally surprising. When the flint of sorrow strikes the steel of the Savior, a spark ignites. And that spark brings light to the darkest situation.

Jesus Hears Our Heartache

Before Jesus ever saw the widow, he *heard* her. A young man is being carried outside of the village to be buried. A crowd of mourners surrounds the bier. The wails of grief sound the alarm of deep sadness. The village is made aware that someone is dead.

How could Jesus be of any assistance in this instance? The young man is gone. Maybe that's why we never hear of the widow calling for Jesus' help. *It's too late.*

When we read the Gospels, we see that Jesus raised three people from the dead:

- The widow's son (Luke 7:11–17)

- Jairus's daughter (Matthew 9:18–26; Mark 5:21–43;
  Luke 8:40–56)

- Lazarus (John 11:38–44)

Jesus raises a young man, a little girl, and a good friend.

But in the cases of Jairus's daughter and Lazarus, Jesus is summoned for help when the little girl is *dying* and when Lazarus is *dying.* They are going to die, but they're not dead when Jesus is called upon to help. The widow's son, on the other hand, is already dead. What could Jesus possibly do when the breath of life is already gone? We see this way of thinking at work in the story of Jairus and his dying daughter. As Jairus kneels at Jesus' feet, begging him to heal his daughter, "some people came from the house of Jairus,

> "The LORD is close to the brokenhearted and saves those who are crushed in spirit." (Psalm 34:18)

the synagogue leader. 'Your daughter is dead,' they said. 'Why bother the teacher anymore?'" (Mark 5:35).

The girl is dead. What could Jesus do now? The grave, they believed, was beyond the reach of Jesus. Perhaps that's why we never hear of the widow of Nain asking for Jesus' help.

It's Not Too Late to Call Out to Jesus

Parents might feel like it's too late when it comes to their children. It's beyond repair. The damage has been done, so they stop calling out for Jesus. *It's too late.*

But what I love about this story is that even though the widow says nothing, Jesus *hears* her broken heart. She utters not a single coherent word, but her sobbing reaches Jesus. And he comes.

Parents must continue to call out to Jesus. If the grief or the stress is so great that they can't even speak, parents can take comfort in knowing that he hears the cries of their heart. And he comes. *He comes.*

Jesus hears the heartache of mothers and fathers. His heart for children and parents isn't surprising. It's *overwhelming.*

Jesus Sees Our Heartache

Jesus also *sees* heartache: "When the Lord saw her, his heart went out to her" (Luke 7:13). The Greek word *splanchnizomai* means "to have compassion and pity; to be affected deeply in one's inner being." Today, the heart is the seat of the emotions. In Jesus' culture, the seat of the emotions was the gut or, more precisely, the bowels. The word describes a visceral response to the sorrow that Jesus saw. He felt it. Right in his gut.

As he steps closer to the village, what does he see? What does a person look like when grief is raw, less than a day old? Fragile. Shaky. Shocked. Broken. Bewildered. Present but not really there. Terrible, irreversible sadness. Quiet tears. Convulsing sobs.

Jesus sees someone so sad and despairing that without skipping a beat, his heart goes out to her. His heart never hesitates to heal the hurt.

This passage gives us a marvelous glimpse of the heart of God. Some people envision God as cold, or they picture him as distant.

Uninvolved. Uninterested in the pain of a parent. Uncaring. Calculated. Maybe even callous.

Jesus Touches Our Heartache

But here Jesus' heart for her heartache cannot be contained. First, he touches the bier, and the grave procession comes to a halt. During a wake or a viewing today, it's not uncommon to kneel before the coffin of the deceased, say a prayer, and maybe place a hand on the edge of the casket. In Jesus' time, that kind of behavior would make a person unclean. One of the reasons tombs were whitewashed was to make them visible to passersby, so they wouldn't stumble upon one and be defiled.

> Whoever touches a human corpse will be unclean for seven days. They must purify themselves with the water on the third day and on the seventh day; then they will be clean. But if they do not purify themselves on the third and seventh days, they will not be clean. If they fail to purify themselves after touching a human corpse, they defile the LORD's tabernacle. They must be cut off from Israel. Because the water of cleansing has not been sprinkled on them, they are unclean; their uncleanness remains on them. (Numbers 19:11–13)

The sound of grief—that sorrowful sobbing—should have been a signal to Jesus to stay clear, because death (and, therefore, defilement) is in his midst.

Instead, the grief draws Jesus closer.

Jesus draws near to *us* in our grief. He doesn't run from it; he runs toward it.

After touching the bier, he speaks and brings the woman's only son back to life: "Young man, I say to you, get up!" (Luke 7:14). Jesus raises him from the dead! At Jesus' command, the young man sits up and begins to talk. He's *alive*.

Who Is Jesus?

Now the crowd sees that Jesus' reach extends to the grave. That begs the question, "Who *is* this guy?" Their minds race back to other resurrection miracles. Who else has done this kind of thing? Educators call this *prior knowledge*. In order to make sense of what we're learning, we relate new information to previous information. The crowds need to "place" Jesus. Their minds start to rewind. When they hit eight hundred and fifty years in the past, something clicks.

> "Praise be to the God and Father of our Lord Jesus Christ, the Father of compassion and the God of all comfort, who comforts us in all our troubles, so that we can comfort those in any trouble with the comfort we ourselves receive from God."
> (2 Corinthians 1:3-4)

Elijah. Elisha. The crowds can now comfortably fit Jesus into the Great Prophet Box. More specifically, it's the Prophet Like Elijah and Elisha Box.

And why shouldn't they? His miracle at Nain mimics those performed by the earlier prophets. Both Elijah and Elisha performed resurrection miracles. In fact, like Jesus, they both raised boys to life (1 Kings 17:17–24; 2 Kings 4:18–37). The first resurrection miracle ever recorded in Scripture was when Elijah resurrected the son of a widow. Jesus' first resurrection miracle is this one—when he raises the widow's son. So it's natural for the crowds to link Jesus to Elijah. God has clearly come to the aid of the widow of Nain. They've determined, therefore, that Jesus is a great prophet sent by God to help them.

Life without a husband and son meant not only a life of loneliness but also a life of poverty. It fell upon children to take care of their parents in their sunset years. Without any descendants, the widow would rely on the help of the community, as required by Mosaic Law. Jews were expected to care for widows, orphans, and the poor.

The people have wept with the widow, and they would have been expected to care for her every need. But instead, Jesus steps in. The crowd is convinced that God is helping his people through Jesus.

And they are confident with how they've pinned Jesus as prophet. John the Baptist, on the other hand, showed he was on shaky ground when he sent two of his disciples to ask Jesus, "Are you the one who is to come, or should we expect someone else?" (Luke 7:20). John expected Jesus to be a bit more than a great prophet. John anticipated the Messiah. Did he get it wrong?

Jesus answered John disciples: "Go back and report to John what you have seen and heard: The blind receive sight, the lame walk, those who have leprosy are cleansed, the deaf hear, the dead are raised, and the good news is proclaimed to the poor" (Luke 7:22).

> "Do not take advantage of the widow or the fatherless. If you do and they cry out to me, I will certainly hear their cry." (Exodus 22:22-23)
>
> "He defends the cause of the fatherless and the widow." (Deuteronomy 10:18)

When those words were reported to John, *his* prior knowledge would have kicked in. Jesus was quoting Isaiah. But not any old passages from Isaiah. He was quoting messianic passages (26:19; 29:18–19; 35:5–6; 42:7, 18; 61:1).

This miracle is important because it's another piece of evidence that the messianic era, or the era of fulfillment, has arrived in Jesus. But even so, Jesus defies traditional messianic expectations. In New Testament times, people expected the Messiah to topple Rome and rule as in the days of King David.

But that's not the gist of Jesus' kingdom. Yes, he has come to save people—but from what? Jesus is getting at the root cause: sin. The crowds rejoice: "God has come to help his people" (Luke 7:16), but they have no idea *how* God has come to help his people; they have no idea *why* God has come to help his people; they have no idea that *God in the flesh* has come to help his people.

A Glimpse of God

The raising of the widow's son gives us a glimpse of what Jesus' kingdom is all about: life. Eternal life. A forgiven-from-sin life. A joyful life. This is a glimpse, a momentary or partial view, of the compassionate heart of God.

Rich and I lived in Scotland for a year. We had a flat in New Town, Edinburgh—on 33 Howe Street, TFR (top, front, right flat). If Rich held me by the waist, I could stick my head, neck, and torso far enough out of the living room window to catch a glimpse of the castle in Old Town.

We called our parents to tell them we had a castle view. Needless to say, they were a wee bit disappointed with our view when they came to visit a few days later. Not one of them dared to thrust their head out the window while Rich secured them from inside.

But we still loved our glimpse. Our sliver.

Days later, when we journeyed into Old Town, the whole castle finally came into view. I couldn't believe my eyes. I was astounded by its enormity and its location right in the midst of the city. But from our flat, we only had a glimpse of something great that rested in the heart of the city.

In some ways, the story of Jesus and the widow of Nain is a glimpse. It's a sliver of something much greater. It's a partial view of God's kingdom. What does this glimpse reveal about God's kingdom? Jesus gives life where there was death.

The most obvious death is the death of the young man. But something also died inside the mother when her son stopped breathing: her hope for the future and her joy in the present.

Her hope for the future was dashed by her son's death, because he was her safety net, her social security. Her daily joy departed from her everyday life. Everything would be experienced differently than it had been before. She wouldn't cook a meal in the same way. She wouldn't sit on her roof or in her doorway and stare into the sunset in the same way. She wouldn't dream about the possibilities of the future in the same way.

Parents who have experienced tragedy understand what it's like to have something die inside of them. They are still breathing, but they're not living.

But one touch from Jesus—God incarnate—and life is reborn. The story is a glimpse of God's power. God, through Jesus, gives life where there was death.

Don't Cry—God Has a Heart for Parents

No big theological reason is given for why Jesus heals the widow's son. But God's relationship to the world is still revealed in this story. We see something very tender about the heart of God: *he sees grieving parents, and his heart goes out to them.*

Jesus has a heart for hurting parents. In this case, it just so happens that his heart goes out to a hurting *mother*. But let's be more precise. In this instance, Jesus' heart goes out to a hurting *single* mom.

She's a widow. Some parents are raising children alone for different reasons. Some *feel* like a single parent, because the bulk of parenting has fallen on their shoulders. Guess what? Those anxious moments, those sleepless nights, those doctor's appointments, those decisions made all alone, those long hours, those years of doing the work of two, those delayed vacations and downsized birthdays and Christmases—*the heart of God goes out to them.* He *sees* them.

God's heart still goes out to all of us today. His *love* goes out to us. That's what the cross is all about. We read in Romans 5:8, "God demonstrates his own love for us in this: While we were still sinners, Christ died for us." The very heart of God—beating, drumming, pumping blood—stopped on the cross. His heart went out to you. His heart went out *for* you. He died for our sin, went to the grave, and conquered sin and death. And his heart still goes out to us as he pours out his love on our wounds, our hurts, and our heartaches.

Yes, Jesus sees parents. He hears mothers and fathers. His heart goes out to them. And that is a reason for rejoicing.

Jesus speaks only two words to this mom: "Don't cry." When you know that Jesus turns death into life, these two words make a lot more sense. We never again have to cry as if hope is lost forever.

How to Make a Scrooge Happy Forever

In the days before Junior died, I had the opportunity to visit him at his bedside. I held his hand. It was warm and strong, even though inside, he was fading away. He was alert, although he had lost the ability to speak.

In the early years of my acquaintance with Junior, he was much more comfortable outside of the church than inside. But as his granddaughter got more involved in our children's ministry, Junior would make an appearance now and then in the sanctuary— usually to listen to her sing or read Scripture. A few years passed, and Junior began brewing the coffee for our fellowship hour, but he kept to the kitchen during the worship service. I don't know exactly when it happened or why it happened, but one Sunday morning, Junior was sitting in the sanctuary. He was there the next Sunday and the Sunday after and the Sunday after that. Junior was a churchgoer!

But sitting by his bedside, I needed to be certain that this churchgoer knew Jesus. I reminded him of the gospel that he heard many times from the cushioned back-row pew. "Jesus died for your sin, Junior. When you put your trust in him, he forgives your sin and gives you a place with him in heaven. Do you trust him to take your sin?" I said.

Junior squeezed my hand, and then he let go. He grinned and gave me his trademark thumbs-up.

Don't cry. Jesus brings life where there is death. The grave is *not* beyond his reach. In fact, nothing is.

SUMMARY

- Mourn with those who mourn. The apostle Paul reminds believers to rejoice with those who rejoice and mourn with those who mourn (Romans 12:15).

- Jesus hears our heartache, and when the grief is so great that we have no words, Jesus hears our heart.

- Jesus sees our heartache and draws near to us in our pain (2 Corinthians 1:3-5).

- Jesus feels our heartache in his gut.

- Jesus is greater than the prophets, for he conquered death.

- God has a heart for all parents, including single parents.

- There's no need to cry hopeless tears: The grave is not beyond the reach of Jesus, and one day, those who trust in him will also rise.

READ

Psalm 121

TAKE ACTION

Identify three ways in which you might come alongside someone who is grieving or who is in the midst of a desperate situation.

PRAY

Heavenly Father,

When my grief is so tender that I can barely utter a sound, you hear the cry of my heart. I'm grateful that you are not a distant God. You walked on this earth. You know what it's like to feel grief and sorrow and pain. Thank you that you know what my pain feels like. And thank you for always having your eye on me. You never fail to see me.

I've experienced grief as a parent. I know what it feels like to not want to cry out to you anymore. Give me the strength to call out to you and the faith to trust that you are there.

I pray for _____ because they feel abandoned. By friends. By family. Even by you, God. Show them that you are always present—seeing, hearing, and feeling. But even more, that you act in our lives. Reveal yourself to _____, so they realize that you care deeply about what is going on.

Thank you, God, that nothing is impossible for you. Even death is not beyond your reach.

Amen.

Questions for Personal Reflection or Group Discussion

1. Describe the most memorable funeral you've attended. What made it so memorable? Was it because the deceased was a close friend or family member? Did it have to do with the service itself? The words spoken? The location? The people in attendance?

2. What are the differences between the way modern people bury their dead and the people in New Testament times? What are the similarities?

3. Thinking of Romans 12:15, how would you have mourned with the widow of Nain? How have you grieved alongside a heartbroken mother or father?

4. Who has been there for you as you've struggled or grieved in your parenting? Has anyone ever grieved with you (cried with you, held your hand, draped an arm over your shoulder, baked goodies, cooked dinner, cleaned house, mowed the lawn, folded laundry, watched the kids, sat silently by your side just so that you wouldn't be alone)? How has this person helped you?

5. As a parent, have you ever been to the point when you've asked, "How can I carry on?" Briefly describe the circumstances.

6. Describe a time in your trial when you felt or knew that Jesus was there with you.

7. Explain your understanding of Jesus' words to the widow: "Don't cry."

8. Read 1 Kings 17:17–24. What are the similarities and differences between the story involving Elijah and the story of the woman from Nain?

9. Explain why you think Jesus' first resurrection miracle mimics Elijah's miracle.

CHAPTER 6

Service Is Greatness

Matthew 20:20–28

Then the mother of Zebedee's sons came to Jesus with her sons and, kneeling down, asked a favor of him.

"What is it you want?" he asked.

She said, "Grant that one of these two sons of mine may sit at your right and the other at your left in your kingdom."

"You don't know what you are asking," Jesus said to them. "Can you drink the cup I am going to drink?"

"We can," they answered.

Jesus said to them, "You will indeed drink from my cup, but to sit at my right or left is not for me to grant. These places belong to those for whom they have been prepared by my Father."

When the ten heard about this, they were indignant with the two brothers. Jesus called them together and said, "You know that the rulers of the Gentiles lord it over them, and their high officials exercise authority over them. Not so with you. Instead, whoever wants to become great among you must be your servant, and whoever wants to be first must be your slave—just as the Son of Man did not come to be served, but to serve, and to give his life as a ransom for many."

What Jesus said to parents:
You don't know what you are asking.

A Mother's Terrible Regret

Only weeks before, Jesus had told the mother of James and John that she didn't know what she was asking.

Now, under the shadow of the cross, on a hill called Golgotha, this woman watches and weeps. The image is too much to bear: a dying Jesus. Upon his mess of dark hair clings a crown of thorns. Its unforgiving branches prick his scalp, sending trickles of blood to streak his cheeks in narrow streams of cruelty. Strands of his hair are matted together in crimson clumps. Above the twisted wreath, a sign mocks him: King of the Jews. That image alone is enough to break anyone. But it's the picture of the *three* crucified men that brings the mother to her knees. One hangs at Jesus' right. The other at his left. The men at the right and left are strangers to the woman. But they could have been her sons. This mother remembers. That day is etched in her mind: she knelt before Jesus with a bold request: "Grant that one of these two sons of mine may sit at your right and the other at your left in your kingdom" (Matthew 20:21). Jesus replied, "You don't know what you are asking" (verse 22).

What had she said? What mother would wish her sons on the right and left of Jesus at that moment?

Under any other circumstance, the right and left were positions of honor. But not that day. Not on the cross. That was the seat of shame.

Passage Prep for Parents

- Name some "interfering" mothers or fathers that you've seen in movies or television shows or heard about in pop culture. How specifically did they interfere?

- Why were the ten disciples indignant with the two brothers (verse 24)?

- If you were the mother of James and John, would you have made that request to Jesus? Why or why not?

- Can you remember a time when one of your parents interfered in your world? Explain the situation and how it made you feel.

- Is there a time that you asked for something, but when it came down to it, you really didn't know what you were asking for? Briefly describe what happened.

Interfering Mothers

Women had few advantages in the ancient world. But older women in particular were allowed one liberty that other people were not. They could get away with saying things that most people wouldn't dare say.[17] In the PBS hit drama *Downton Abbey*, Violet Crawley, Dowager Countess of Grantham, admits without apology, "It is the job of grandmothers to interfere."

I have been more shocked by the statements that come from the mouths of senior women than I have from the words that fall off the lips of teenagers.

Helen wasn't five feet tall, but she had a mighty personality. She drove a red Ford that she referred to as "Jimmy." She had a heart as big as a Mack Truck. And she had a mouth like a truck driver.

She was a Kennebunkport, Maine, crossing guard. She kept the corner of School Street and Maine Street safe, guarding it with her metal Stop sign and a shrill shout at cars and people who didn't follow the rules. She was a four-foot ten-inch force. It didn't matter who she spoke to. She didn't change her manner—whether you were a truck driver traveling down the street or a little kid crossing the road or the Bush presidential motorcade whizzing past the corner. She held no prejudices. She'd yell at anyone. And I absolutely adored that woman.

Helen could get away with it. Much of that was due to her age.

A Mother's Plan

The mother of James and John makes explicit what is hidden in the minds of everyone else. In other words, she's the only one with the nerve to ask.

She wants the best for her boys, and she feels pressure to make a move quickly, because Jesus has been talking a lot about his coming kingdom. And it seems imminent.

From her perspective, it's clear that her two sons, James and John, have risen to the top of the disciple pack. Peter was right up there, too. Every so often, Jesus pulled these three former fishermen aside for excursions apart from the others.

Peter, this mother knew, was a real contender for a leadership position. He had recently said to Jesus, "We have left everything to follow you! What then will there be for us?" (Matthew 19:27).

Jesus answered him, "Truly I tell you, at the renewal of all things, when the Son of Man sits on his glorious throne, you who have followed me will also sit on twelve thrones, judging the twelve tribes of Israel" (Matthew 19:28).

Hmm…twelve thrones? Without pause, the wheels started turning in dear old Mom's mind. How would these thrones be arranged?

Perhaps she imagined a typical setup at a meal. A table was configured in a U shape. At the curve of the U reclined the most honored person. To his right was the second most honored. To his left, the next honored, and so on and so forth, all the way to the end of the table.[18] Her son John was often seated directly to the right of Jesus. They were the closest of friends, and he was referred to as "the disciple whom Jesus loved" (John 13:23; 21:7, 20).

The Seat of Honor

Jesus talked a lot about his kingdom. Naturally, he would be king of his kingdom. But who would be his right-hand man? The seat to the right of the king was a position of power and influence. The Jewish historian Josephus said that the eldest son of the king sits to the right and the commander of the army sits to the left of the king.[19] Or, for a more modern twist on right and left, think of the State of the Union address, which is delivered in the House chamber in the Capitol each January. The president stands front and center. To his right is the vice president and to the president's left is the speaker of the house. They are, respectively, second and third in line to the office, should something happen to the president.

Of course, any advantage to her sons would be an advantage to her and her husband, Zebedee, as well. Surely Jesus would reign from the holy city, Jerusalem. Maybe Zebedee could finally sell the fishing business in Capernaum. They could move south to Jerusalem for their sunset years. All of that could be sorted out later. But for now, she needed to secure the top two spots for her sons. She'd deal with the details later. After all, it was the job of the parent to interfere.

She hatched a plan with James and John. They would get to Jesus before the others. Kneeling down, she asked Jesus if he would grant a favor. "What is it you want?" Jesus replied (verse 21). She said, "Grant that one of these two sons of mine may sit at your right and the other at your left in your kingdom" (verse 22).

Jesus didn't give a definitive yes or no or even a let-me-think-on-it. Instead, he said, "You don't know what you are asking.… Can you drink the cup I am going to drink?" (verse 24).

Our youngest son makes his birthday list months in advance. It changes over the weeks, so the scooter he wanted in February is out in March, and the Lego set is in. He often asks for items that are well beyond his capabilities or even the realm of sanity. Although he was still riding with training wheels, he wanted a ten-speed bicycle. He frequently asks for lions and tigers and bears (oh my). Real, live, breathing ones. When he realized the animal route was closed, he was off to the army. "Can we buy a tank?" he once asked. His brothers rolled their eyes and said, "Where would we even put a tank?" as if that's the main problem with a civilian buying a fully outfitted military-grade tank for a four-year-old! "What about a cannon?" he asked. When I shook my head no, he complained, "Come on. You don't let me have anything!" After reviewing the list, a ten-speed for a four-year-old doesn't sound that bad. But I'm not giving in on the tank or the lion!

The fact of the matter is that he doesn't know what he's asking. Sometimes we don't either.

This mother's plea wasn't in line with Jesus' program. It was all about her plan. Her program. For herself. For her children.

The surprising thing was that Jesus talked about the nature of his kingdom *a lot*. And thrusting oneself into the limelight of glory and honor wasn't part of citizenship in his kingdom.

Once, when Jesus was eating at the home of a Pharisee, he noticed how the guests picked the places of honor at the table. Imagine these grown men and women, scurrying about, trying to secure honor by snatching up a good seat, while trying to maintain their dignity at the same time.

Aisle Hog Honor

Every January, the president of the United States delivers the annual State of the Union speech. The House chamber is packed with senators, representatives, US Supreme Court justices, cabinet members, dignitaries, and special guests. Very few seats, however, are actually reserved. Senate and House leaders have a reserved section. Supreme Court justices and a few others do as well. But when it comes to rank and file House members, it's general admission. It's a free-for-all. They can save seats during the day, but in order to retain the seat, they must be sitting in it.[20] No placards or purses strewn across the seats for substitutes. Let's face it: we've all witnessed this behavior at school concerts. And at some point, we've probably participated in it.

Some House members have earned the title Aisle Hog by making sure they have the best seat in the house—the one that will come closest to crossing paths with the president, the seat that will ensure a selfie or a handshake with the commander-in-chief.

But Jesus says:

> When someone invites you to a wedding feast, do not take the place of honor, for a person more distinguished than you may have been invited. If so, the host who invited both of you will come and say to you, "Give this man your seat." Then, humiliated, you will have to take the least important place. But when you are invited, take the lowest place, so that when your host comes, he will say to you, "Friend, move up to a better place." Then you will be honored in the presence of all the other guests. For all those who exalts themselves will be humbled, and those who humble themselves will be exalted. (Luke 14:8–11)

Me First!

So often we see our kids clamoring to be first. As Timmy's pre-K Sunday school class was coming to a close, Miss Marie was setting out an assortment of goodies at the other end of the fellowship hall. The three- and four-year-olds could barely sit still during the ending prayer. When the amen "bell" finally rang off the lips of the teacher, the kids bolted for the food table like bats out of the belfry. Halfway down the tile floor, the teacher yelled, "Stop!" Every single one of those kids came to a complete halt. "Come back and write your names on your paper!" Those obedient little soldiers marched back to their artwork. All except one. Timmy yelled from the halfway mark, "Mine will be the one without the name on it!" Then he raced to the food table where he was first in line.

Parents know how refreshing it is when their child chooses to be last. Yes, there's parental pride in first place. But there's even more pride when your child chooses humility.

Humility Jackpot

My middle son told me about a game the kids play at recess. It's called Jackpot. One child begins by standing on a hill. He or she faces away from a whole crowd of children who wait at the bottom of the hill with hands raised. The chosen child throws a ball overhead to the crowd below. (Yes, think of a bride tossing her bouquet.) Of course, nobody knows exactly where it will land. Everyone scrambles to catch it. The one who snatches it up then gets to toss the ball. A few of the older, bigger kids snag the ball every single time. Sam, who is above average height for his age, decided to stand in the middle of the crowd and claim the prize in order to give it to one of the younger, smaller kids so that they would have a chance to throw the ball. He played until every smaller kid had a turn throwing the ball.

Last Is First and First Is Last

Maybe what my son did doesn't sound like a big deal to most people, but it is to God. This little boy demonstrated the characteristics of a kingdom person: the first shall be last and the last shall be first. He caught the jackpot and gave it away.

Matthew recorded Jesus' first words about the first being last and the last being first in chapter 19. Peter asks Jesus, "What then will there be for us?" (verse 27). Jesus answers him by talking about the renewal of all things, the Son of Man sitting on his throne, and his followers sitting on twelve thrones to judge the twelve tribes of Israel (verse 28). Then Jesus says, "And everyone who has left houses or brothers or sisters or father or mother or wife or children or fields for my sake will receive a hundred times as much and will inherit eternal life. But many who are first will be last, and many who are last will be first" (Matthew 19:29–30).

Then Jesus tells the parable of the workers in the vineyard (Matthew 20:1–16). The men who were hired early in the morning and worked under the heat of the sun made the same amount of money as the men who only worked a couple of hours in the shade of the afternoon. Jesus concludes the parable by saying, "So the last will be first, and the first will be last."

There are people who are "first" in this life, and everything they do revolves around being first. The first in line at the food table. The top spot on the team. The head honcho. But Jesus says if being first is your priority in this world, then in his kingdom, you are really last.

Serving Is Greatness

Serving others in this life is what matters in the next life. Service on earth is greatness in heaven.

Imagine if parents tweaked their prayers for their children. Instead of asking God to make their kids great on earth, they'd ask God to make their kids great in heaven. That doesn't mean parents don't want them to do their best or don't want them to succeed on earth. It means the primary focus of parents in this world is raising kids to serve God and serve others.

Why should this be the focus of parents? Because it's the very reason Jesus came into the world.

After James's and John's mother makes the request, the rest of the disciples get wind of it, and they are mad. Why are they angry? Possibly because James and John thought so highly of themselves. But it's more likely they are upset because they hadn't thought of going to Jesus first. James and John and their mother had beaten them to the punch.

Jesus then takes the opportunity to gather his disciples in like a hen with her chicks. He reminds them how power structures work in the world. Rulers lord power and position over their people. But Jesus says that his kingdom doesn't work that way: "Not so with you. Instead, whoever wants to become great among you must be your servant, and whoever wants to be first must be your slave—just as the Son of Man did not come to be served, but to serve, and to give his life as a ransom for many" (Matthew 20:26–28).

In God's kingdom, greatness means service.

There's no greater model of servanthood than Jesus. He came into the world to serve us by giving his life as a ransom. We are all held captive to sin. Jesus bought us out of captivity. He paid the ransom with his life. That is service of the highest calling. It's greatness.

Drinking the Cup of Christ

As the mother of James and John wept beneath the cross, she probably recalled Jesus' question to her boys that day: "Can you drink the cup I am going to drink?" (verse 22). The "cup" meant *suffering*. Jesus asked James and John if they are able to endure great suffering. They both say yes. Jesus replies, "You will indeed drink from my cup" (verse 23).

Beneath the cross, her request hung like an albatross around her neck. At the foot of the cross, Jesus' reply haunted her. He had been right; she had had no idea what she was asking. What had she done? I imagine she couldn't let go of that conversation as she watched Jesus die.

Many parents have moments that they keep replaying. They wish they could take them back or do them over.

Church history tells us that James was one of the first followers to be martyred for Jesus when Herod put him to the sword (Acts 12:2). John, on the other hand, lived a long life. But he lived in exile, on the isle of Patmos. He wrote a gospel as well as letters. He saw visions of the future and recorded them on parchment; we know those writings as Revelation.

Their mother must have endured enormous suffering. One son sentenced to death in his prime; the other, exiled far from home. That's not what she had in mind when she approached Jesus that day.

But after the resurrection, everything changed, because then she knew what it meant to be great in God's eyes. It meant service and sacrifice. And what she looked like in God's eyes was all that mattered. She remembered Jesus' words to her sons: "You will indeed drink from my cup." But now, she knew fully what that meant. She realized exactly whom she and they served—God Almighty. Any sacrifice they made on the Lord's behalf was nothing compared to the sacrifice he had made for them. How her children served the Lord—that's what's important to God, and that's what should be important to her. And it's true that her sons were called to radical service and sacrifice—but she knew that Christ had gone before them, and he would be with them no matter what happened. The empty tomb shed new light on her situation.

Her children lived and died for Jesus, the resurrected Lord. They served him and his purposes in the world. They promoted God's plan wherever they went. In God's eyes, they were great.

Parents, raise *great* kids.

SUMMARY

- The mother of John and James wanted greatness for her children.

- Greatness, according to Jesus, means service.

- Jesus served us in the ultimate way.

- Parents are wise when they raise biblically great kids.

READ

Matthew 18:1–5

TAKE ACTION

Read Matthew 20:20–28 with your children. Ask them what it means to be great in God's eyes. Do they have a specific example of a time when they were great during the week?

Identify a service project with your kids. Take time to plan it and build enthusiasm. Then, go forth and serve! Talk about what each person learned.

PRAY

Dear God,

I admit that I pray more for my children's safety than I do for their service. I've invested time and money and energy into their earthly greatness. Help me to invest in greatness from your perspective.

Show us how to serve you as a family.

I think I understand some of what it means to be a servant. I serve my family day in and day out. I don't always do it cheerfully, Lord. Give me your perspective as I serve my family. Show me how what I'm doing as I serve may not be great in the eyes of the world, but it is great in your eyes. Help me to care about what matters to you, God.

I pray for my children, _____. I pray that you would give them opportunities to choose humility rather than pride. Give them opportunities to put others first. Give them the chance to serve. Give them the chance to be great in your eyes.

Amen.

Questions for Personal Reflection or Group Discussion

1. Do you really want God's idea of greatness first and foremost for your children? What is preventing you from desiring that first?

2. How can you practically invest in your kids' godly greatness?

3. Write down an example of a time when your child demonstrated godly greatness. Don't overlook small acts of service and don't forget to tell your child how important their act of service was.

4. What things/acts are "great" in our world? Make a list of things/ acts that are "great" in heaven.

5. If you were a disciple on the scene, which one would you be—one of the ten indignant disciples or one of the brothers who made the request? Give a reason for your choice.

6. Can you describe a situation in your life when you (or someone else) asked for something that upset other people, who maybe wished that they asked first?

CHAPTER 7

Issues of the Heart

John 2:1–11

On the third day a wedding took place at Cana in Galilee. Jesus' mother was there, and Jesus and his disciples had also been invited to the wedding. When the wine was gone, Jesus' mother said to him, "They have no more wine."

"Woman, why do you involve me?" Jesus replied. "My hour has not yet come."

His mother said to the servants, "Do whatever he tells you."

Nearby stood six stone water jars, the kind used by the Jews for ceremonial washing, each holding from twenty to thirty gallons.

Jesus said to the servants, "Fill the jars with water"; so they filled them to the brim.

Then he told them, "Now draw some out and take it to the master of the banquet."

They did so, and the master of the banquet tasted the water that had been turned into wine. He did not realize where it had come from, though the servants who had drawn the water knew. Then he called the bridegroom aside and said, "Everyone brings out the choice wine first and then the cheaper wine after the guests have had too much to drink; but you have saved the best till now."

What Jesus did here in Cana of Galilee was the first of the signs through which he revealed his glory; and his disciples believed in him.

What Jesus said to parents:
Woman...

Hey, Mom!

We have a tween in the house. He's not quite a teenager, but he's not a little boy either. On Wednesday nights he stays up past his bedtime and watches a television show with Rich and me. After the little kids are sleeping, the three of us cram into the "big bed." Wedged between us and nestled into a stack of pillows is our tween. Rich and I wonder how much longer he'll want to snuggle into the comfort of Mom and Dad's bed.

Our job as parents, of course, is to raise a child into a full-fledged, decision-making adult. I know that. But somehow, as I see my kids grow, my heart is pierced, because I know the relationship will change. You can hear the progression in the relationship just by the way kids address us, their parents.

When our kids were learning to talk, they called me Mama. Now it's Mom. The oldest will often refer to me as Mother, just to irritate me. "That's a bit formal," I say. The little one, who still replaces the letter *r* with a *w*, breaks out into hysterical laughter and says, "Okay, *mothew*."

In John 2:1–11, we learn that Jesus uses a rather formal term when addressing his mother. He calls her "Woman." But he's not joking around, and I imagine it caught Mary a bit off guard.

By his use of the word *woman*, Jesus is indicating something important about their mother-son relationship. It's something that must have pierced Mary's soul, and it's something that will pierce every mother's soul.

Passage Prep for Parents

- Turning water into wine is Jesus' first recorded miracle. What do you think the significance is in regard to the event (a wedding) and the substance of the miracle (water into wine)? Or do you not see any significance?

- What do you think ceremonial washing was all about?

- What is Mary's role in this first miracle?

- Name the probable results of Jesus' miracle. (Don't forget to look at verse 11.)

Mary as Mother

In many ways, Mary's experience as a mother wasn't much different from any mother's experience. She remembered all of those "firsts": Jesus' first step—his four small fingers and a pudgy thumb wrapped around her index finger as if his life depended on it. Then he let go. Shaky. Wobbly. But independent.

His first fall still sent shudders down her spine. She had tended to his scraped knees and those bumps on the forehead that she had thought might never go down. Scooping him up in her arms, Mary had wiped away his tears.

She remembered the first time she lost track of him (Luke 2:41–50). The frantic shouts: "Jesus! Jesus!" The weaving in and out of a crowd of people—a sea of robes and tunics and sandals, hoping to spot the ones that matched her son's. Three sleepless nights. Searching.

In many ways, Mary's experience of motherhood was similar to that of any twenty-first-century mom.

But in other ways, it wasn't at all. Some parents today might describe their children as gifted, but when it comes to exceptional kids, Mary hit the jackpot. Moms in this century watch their child's first hit at bat or their dancing debut. They can still picture their child's leg stretching as their little one stepped onto that first step on the school bus. It was all caught on a camcorder or an iPhone. Mary watched her son's first *miracle*. She captured it in her heart.

Raising Jesus

Mary always knew that Jesus was different, starting from the time the angel Gabriel visited her with the news that she'd bear the Messiah—a virgin birth (Luke 1:26–38). She remembered the visit from the shepherds (Luke 2:8–20) and the wise men (Matthew 2:1–12); she remembered the prophecies of Simeon and Anna (Luke 2:22–38). Mary knew her son was a gift from God. He was different. He was capable of great things. He was resourceful. He was close to God. But Mary had never before seen him do what he did in Cana that day. It was his first miracle.

Wedding Stress

Weddings and the parties that usually follow are carefully choreographed events. That was true in ancient times, and it's true today. Guests attend these events with certain expectations. Sometimes, to the delight of all, expectations are exceeded, and the wedding reception is a huge success. Other times, expectations are not met, and guests leave disappointed. In New Testament times, when a wedding reception didn't meet the standard, the family of the groom would not only be shamed but could also face a lawsuit![21]

Wedding Expectations

Attending a wedding is an investment. In money. In time. You need the right shoes, the right dress, the right accessories.

Hair and makeup must look good. Sometimes attendance at a wedding requires travel and hotel expenses. Weddings also take time. Usually several hours.

A couple planned a Coca-Cola and pie wedding reception. The guests, however, were not aware that lunch would not be served. After enduring a mid-morning service lasting ninety minutes, the guests were expecting to munch on something of substance—chips, or cheese and crackers; peanuts, or pigs in a blanket. But all they were offered was another round of Coca-Cola and another slice of pecan pie. A few hours into the festivities, crashing from sugar shock, guests were hungry and irritable.

Wedding Hospitality

Years ago, I officiated a summer wedding in a quaint but cramped chapel. Guests were packed into creaky wooden benches like kids at a school assembly. The bride was an hour late. I learned later that she had had a make-up malfunction. Was her husband-to-be aware of her impolite propensity for perfection? If not, he had sixty minutes to figure it out.

The string quartet played Brahms and Bach and Handel and Haydn. Then they played Mozart and Rachmaninoff. Then they turned to contemporary music: Lionel Richie, Barbara Streisand, and Stevie Wonder. I tried to think of something positive in this dire situation. The only thankful thought I could muster was that bagpipes had not been assigned to the prelude. Then the violinist packed up her instrument and prepared to charge out the door. Guests fidgeted. Little boys and grown men who were not accustomed to wearing dress shirts and ties and jackets shifted uneasily in their seats. They tucked and tugged at their cotton-polyester-blend prisons. Some indeed broke free. Women fanned themselves with the wedding program. Someone opened a window. The allergy sufferers sneezed when the pollen was caught up in the breeze. The groom and his groomsmen wiped sweat from their brows with tuxedo handkerchiefs. Everyone was on edge.

When the bride finally graced us with her presence, a collective sigh of irritated relief filled the room. The bride did not receive the warm welcome that most do as they walk the aisle on their wedding day. Had she not overlooked her guests, they might have demonstrated a different response.

Yes, weddings are about the bride and the groom. But they are also about the guests and showing them hospitality.

Mary and Jesus and his disciples were at a wedding feast in the town of Cana, about nine miles north of their hometown of Nazareth. The bridegroom had already walked with his party to the home of the bride. At night, in a procession of light, the torches illuminated the dark sky. The party escorted the bride and her bridesmaids back to the bridegroom's home, and a wedding celebration commenced that lasted a week!

Mary assisted with banquet preparations—perhaps washing cups and baking bread and roasting meat. The aroma of roasted lamb filled the house, wafting into the street. A seven-day feast was no small task. The celebration was the responsibility of the bridegroom and his family.

It was getting close to the end of the celebration when Mary noticed the supply of wine was dreadfully low.

Running out of food or wine at a celebration is a huge headache. Imagine running out of hotdogs at Fenway Park or popcorn at the movies. Running out of wine during the wedding feast would be a major embarrassment to the bridegroom and his family. It wasn't the right way to start a marriage. One would certainly lose honor.

Wanting to protect this family's honor, Mary approached her son, Jesus. "They have no more wine," she said (John 2:3).

A Mom Who Had a Way with Words

There are some parents who excel in the art of subtlety. They might not come right out and say, "Would you help in this situation?" Instead, they come at it indirectly—"There's no more wine." *Ahem.* Sometimes this light touch helps. Sometimes it contributes to miscommunication or frustration.

Of course, Jesus got her meaning. And he said something that changed their relationship. Forever. He said, "Woman."

Woman? Really?

A Son's Rebuke

There certainly were more affectionate terms Jesus could have used in addressing his mother. This was not the typical way a son would talk to his much-loved mother.[22] So why did he call her "Woman"?

The rest of the phrase gives us some insight: "Woman, why do you involve me?" This phrase is tricky, even for Bible translators, and most translations soften it. The literal translation is "what to me and to you?" It means, *what do you and I have in common?* or *you have no claims on me.* It's a phrase that, in effect, puts distance between the two parties involved and is seen as a "measured rebuke."[23]

This sounds like the snide remark of a snarky teenager who is trying to create distance between themselves and their parents in order to gain a little independence. Why on earth would Jesus ever use such a phrase with his mother? Surely, it pierced Mary's soul.

A Changing Relationship

It was as if Jesus were saying, "You expect me to do something in this situation on the basis of our relationship—mother-son. But the primary relationship is me and my Father—my heavenly Father. What I do, I do in terms of *that* relationship."

My kids often ask, "What's the plan for today?" I rattle off a list of errands and chores. After some negotiation, they begrudgingly submit to my will. But *I* set the itinerary. *I* make the plan.

Mary was still making the list. She didn't realize that Jesus was in charge of writing the list.

We went through it with our parents, and we're seeing it happen with our kids. The relationship changes. We are no longer the primary person in the relationship—friends become more important; later, maybe a husband or a wife takes over that primary spot. For Jesus, it was his relationship with his heavenly Father.

It's hard for a mother to give up that primary spot. But let's face it: Jesus' relationship with his heavenly Father went *way* back. John talks about it in the prologue of his book.

Father and Son

Jesus was with God from the very beginning. There was never a time when Jesus didn't exist. Jesus is God the Son, who exists eternally with God the Father and God the Spirit. In John's gospel—the one that records this incident—John talked about Jesus as the Logos: the Word.

What did he mean by "the Word"? A word is an expression of thought. A word expresses what we think in our minds.

When God's Word is involved, action takes place. In the beginning, "God said, 'Let there be light,' and there was light" (Genesis 1:3). He created all that we see by his Word. The Word is the agent of creation. God's Word is his creative action in the world. When God says, God does. God's Word does what he has determined in his mind. God's Word is Jesus—God the Son.

Jesus wasn't some new creation of God's two thousand years ago. Jesus was always the Word. But two thousand years ago, that Word became flesh and lived among people. God incarnate. "The Word became flesh and blood, and moved into the neighborhood" (MSG). That Word became flesh…became Mary's son, and he moved into the neighborhood. He moved into Nazareth.

That's when Mary's relationship began with Jesus—those three decades—when the Word became flesh and blood and moved into the neighborhood. And when God became flesh and blood, he moved through the neighborhoods and touched people and loved people. He shared their laughter and their losses. Their concerns became his concerns. And that's true today. The concerns of parents today are his concerns. In Cana, the bridegroom was running out of wine.

"In the beginning was the Word, and the Word was with God, and the Word was God." (John 1:1)

Perhaps parents today are running out of patience or time or money or stamina or enthusiasm or love or avenues to pursue or ideas.

What concerns parents right now, at this moment, concerns Jesus just as much as he was concerned two thousand years ago, when he walked among people—flesh and blood—sat at a wedding, maybe saw the bridegroom turn pale, and turned water into wine.

Mom Submits to Son

As we've seen so many other parents do throughout the Gospels, Mary perseveres, even when Jesus says something surprising. She doesn't fully understand what he means by his "hour" (verse 4), but she has faith that he will do what is right when it is right. She is no longer trying to manipulate the situation. She is no longer setting the agenda. Mary turns to the servants and leaves it in Jesus' hands: "Do whatever he tells you," she says to them (verse 5).

This is not an okay-fine-have-it-your-way-Jesus kind of response. She is learning to trust him…just like *parents today* must learn to trust him.

Clean Hands

Jesus tells the servants to fill the jars. There were six of them, located outside the entrance of the home. They each held twenty to thirty gallons of water. They were used for ceremonial cleansing. I'm not talking about soap and water and sanitizer like we use today. Ancient people didn't cleanse like that back then. This was a *religious* cleansing. It's not about cleanliness. It's about godliness.

Throughout the day, different things that Jews came in contact with made them ceremonially unclean. To be ceremonially unclean meant you couldn't worship. You were forbidden to enter the synagogue. Coming in contact with a dead body made you unclean. Touching certain kinds of food made a person unclean. Rubbing the robe of the wrong kind of person made you unclean. There were things all over the place that could make a person unclean. The jars were there so that everyone could wash and be purified from external things that made them unclean.

It may sound bizarre to us in the twenty-first century, but the Jews made a life out of it. They built a whole system of living around it, and all Jews were born into the system of ceremonial cleansing. But for many, they had done this practice so often, so routinely, that they had forgotten how or why it had all started in the first place.

How did this tenacious washing start? With a desire to please God. It started with a desire to act on his Word. We read in Psalm 24: "Who may ascend the mountain of the Lord? Who may stand in his holy place? The one who has clean hands and a pure heart." (verses 3–4). In layman's terms, the psalm says those with clean hands and hearts are the only ones who can be in God's presence.

Clean hands was something tangible. But a clean heart…how do you clean a heart? There *is* no way to clean a heart! Jews recognized that only God could do that. But clean hands *was* something every Jewish person could do. So they focused on what they could actually achieve. Thus, ceremonial cleansing started with a desire to please God, a desire to be in his presence. And for some, it *was* that. But for many others, this cleansing of the hands simply became part of the routine, the ritual.

Old Way, New Way

Jesus tells the servants to fill the jars used for ceremonial cleansing. They fill them to the brim. Then Jesus says that some water should be drawn and given to the chief servant. It seems as if the water is drawn from the jars, but it's more likely that the water is drawn from a well. The word used for "drawn" is typically used when referring to drawing water specifically *from a well.*

Why is that significant?

The old system of purification and ceremonial cleansing had reached its limit. It had been fulfilled. The jars were filled full with water, filled to the brim. It was time for something new. It was time for the messianic age, which was characterized by the coming of the Messiah and the ushering in of God's kingdom. Old Testament prophets often referred to the messianic age as a time in which wine flowed liberally. And in Matthew's gospel, Jesus talks about the wedding as a symbol of the fulfillment of the messianic age.[24]

Jesus is replacing the old system with something better. He's replacing water with wine. Up to this point, the servants had been drawing water for ceremonial cleansing. Now, they will begin drawing water for the feast that symbolized the messianic banquet.

Clean Heart

We don't know the precise time the water turned into wine—but by the time it reached the lips of the chief servant, it was the best he had ever tasted. And that was Jesus' very first miracle. It wasn't particularly dramatic or public. But he made something new. Something that could be enjoyed. Something that symbolized the new kind of kingdom he was ushering in.

With that first miracle, it was almost as if Jesus is saying: "This is what I'm all about. I'm taking your ceremonial rituals—that water in the jar—and I'm replacing it with something superior. You try to cleanse yourself with water, but I'll show you that cleansing comes through my blood. You think what's on the outside makes you unclean, but I'll show you that it's what's in your heart that makes you unclean. You purify yourself by washing your hands, but I'll purify you by stretching out my hands."

And on that wretched day when his hands were stretched out on the cross, Jesus addressed Mary again from that crucifixion rack in the same way he addressed her at Cana—"Woman" (John 19:26).

In those dark hours, when Jesus called out to Mary in the crowd, I imagine she remembered the first time he called her *Woman*, right before he performed his first miracle. It was the day their relationship changed. Mary must have been comforted to know it wasn't just the son of Mary dying on the cross; it was the Son of God—dying for sin.

Jesus cleanses our hearts.

And you know what? That makes me feel good. It gives me peace. Because I've made a lot of mistakes. And the ones that sometimes haunt me the most are the mistakes I've made as a parent.

One summer day, the kids and I took a leisurely stroll around the boardwalk. The younger boys took in the sights from the double stroller. The oldest walked. We meandered along the water and picked up pinecones. The kids collect them every year. I can't tell you the number of times I've felt a tug on my shirt and heard, "Is this a good one, Mom?" When Christmas rolls around, we unpack our summer stash and place them on the mantle.

After our bag was full, we got ice cream and sat down on a shady bench. I remember really enjoying the kids that day. I chased them and hugged them and laughed with them.

I had no idea that I had been the object of a people-watching expedition.

As I packed up the kids and headed to the car, an older couple stopped me and said, "You are such a good mother." They caught me being good! I felt a deep sense of parental satisfaction.

Until we got home.

And good mommy was nowhere to be found. Why does she disappear like that?

The house was a disaster. I had to cook supper, take out the dogs, wipe a rear-end, find the wipes, pick up the wipes that were all over the floor because the dog yanked them out of the package, and break up a fight with a mess of dirty wipes in my hand.

I raised my voice. I stomped my foot. I grunted and sighed. I yelled at the top of my lungs. I lacked clean hands and a clean heart. If that couple had seen me, they would have retracted their praise. They might have said, "You are a terrible mom." But they didn't see me. They didn't catch me being bad.

But God did.

My kids did, too.

I think of all the times that I haven't measured up as a mom, and I'm grateful that Jesus cleanses my heart.

Jesus cleanses the hearts of parents. He forgives all of our parenting blunders: our bungled bloopers and our muddled mess-ups, our faults and our flubs, our slipups and our sin.

Parents need to hear that phrase "You are a good mother" or "You are a good father." Not because parents are perfect. But because parents are forgiven.

SUMMARY

- Jesus is concerned about the concerns of parents.

- Water into wine, Jesus' first recorded miracle, signifies the start of something new—the Messiah has come.

- Jesus' first recorded miracle also signifies a new relationship between him and his mother, Mary.

- Ceremonial cleansing became ritual without meaning for many people.

- Jesus cleans hearts and forgives sin, including the sin of parents.

READ

John 1

TAKE ACTION

Catch another parent being good. Tell them what you see that is good about their parenting.

PRAY

Dear God,

Thank you for cleansing my heart. I'm grateful for your forgiveness. You know how I struggle with parenting. I'm prone to impatience and flares of temper. If you caught me doing anything, it would probably be complaining, even though I have so much for which to be grateful.

Show me how to navigate the years when the relationship with my children changes. May we be gentle with each other and always seek your agenda.

Forgive me for _____.

I pray that you would catch me being good far more than you catch me being bad.

Change me. Like Mary, help me to submit to your plan.

Watch over my kids as they grow. I want them to please you and do your will. Give them clean hands and clean hearts.

Amen.

Questions for Personal Reflection or Group Discussion

1. Do you have a story of a wedding or reception that didn't meet expectations? What are the highlights of the story?

2. Have you ever been hurt by something that your son or daughter said to you? Describe the situation.

3. In what ways have you experienced the relationship changing with your children?

4. Do you have a routine with God? Have you ever done something in order to draw yourself closer to God, but your routine was so ingrained that you couldn't remember why you were doing something different in the first place? Briefly describe your routine and what happened when you tried to do something different?

5. Explain the significance of Jesus turning water into wine. What does it have to do with the start of the messianic age?

6. How do you think the groom and his family felt when they learned that they had not run out of wine and that, in fact, the best wine was only now being served?

Acknowledgments

When a book is still in its early stages and the heart of the writer is fragile, inviting people to join the writing journey takes a good dose of courage. The path from private to public is made incrementally as more and more people are included in sharing and shaping the story.

I'm grateful for many people who supported me along this writing adventure. You gave me courage and confidence to share with other parents the hope and mercy found in God's Word.

From the bottom of my heart I thank my mom who sat on the family room rug, building Lego creations with the boys while I wrote. And to my dad, a poet at heart, who beamed with pride at my manuscript.

My grandfather Skeets proved to be a faithful listener and an adept question-asker. At the age of ninety-six, he demonstrated a keen interest in every stage of the project and a deep love for me.

My sisters, Sandy and Karen, provided expertise and humor from the front lines of education and parenting. Maureen, my mother-in-law, has poured courage into Rich and me with the words, "You are good parents."

I owe a debt of gratitude to my church family at Community Congregational in Billerica, Massachusetts. They raised me in the faith from the time I was an infant. Then they invited me to raise them in the faith as their pastor. The ideas in this book were tested in the lives of these faithful men and women.

Considerable thanks goes to my agent, Dan Balow, who championed my proposal and continued to support me throughout the publishing process. The team at Rose Publishing was outstanding. Lynnette Pennings and Kay ben Avraham offered thoughtful feedback and presented it with grace. The book is better because of them.

I value the chapter feedback that Lauren Gagnon provided, and I cherish our conversations about faith and parenting.

Thanks to Kate and Andy Bauer for allowing me to share a glimpse of their story. My heart goes out to them as they navigate life and ministry while being thrust into the world of pediatric cancer.

I'm grateful to Sally Bridges and Village Baptist Church in Kennebunkport, Maine. Ministering to those hearty souls in both life and death was a high privilege that will not be forgotten.

Most important is my husband, Rich. He is a rock. He is the Batten family bard—a master bedtime storyteller. A man of faith and integrity, he has been selfless in his support of me. His commitment to raising the kids in the faith is unwavering.

Before a book is made public, it is private and personal—an idea in the mind of the author. But it's an idea that the writer is convinced will benefit others once it is shared. I hope that by sharing God's Word with you, your faith will flourish as you discover what Jesus said to parents. To God be the glory.

Notes

1. This pattern of Jesus only healing Gentiles from a distance is evident specifically in the synoptic gospel accounts.

2. The phrase *Son of David* refers to a descendant of David whom God will place on a throne to rule his kingdom. The name *David* is given to no one else in the Bible "except the great king of Israel." H. A. White, "David," *A Dictionary of the Bible: Dealing with Its Language, Literature, and Contents, Including the Biblical Theology*, ed. James Hastings, et al. 3 vols. (New York: Charles Scribner's Sons, 1911), 1:560.

3. The word used here is κυνάριον, meaning "small dog," as opposed to κύων, the despised street dog. Frederick William Danker, et al, *A Greek-English Lexicon of the New Testament and Other Early Christian Literature*, 3rd ed. (Chicago: University of Chicago Press, 2000), 575.

4. "The language Jesus uses is very strong. Dogs in Middle Eastern traditional culture, Jewish and non-Jewish, are almost as despised as pigs…. Dogs are never pets. They are kept as half-wild guard dogs or left to wander unattended as dangerous street scavengers who subsist on garbage." Kenneth E. Bailey, *Jesus through Middle Eastern Eyes: Cultural Studies in the Gospels* (Downers Grove, IL: IVP Academic, 2008), 224.

5. Ibid.

6. "Ancient Synagogues," *NIV Archaeological Study Bible: An Illustrated Walk through Biblical History and Culture*, ed. Walter C. Kaiser, Jr. and Duane A. Garrett (Grand Rapids: Zondervan, 2005), 1783.

7. "Those in attendance were seated according to age and status (cf. Mt 23:6; Lk 20:46), and the entire congregation was orientated toward the Most Holy Place in Jerusalem (cf. 1Ki 8:48)." "Ancient Synagogues," *NIV Archaeological Study Bible*, 1783.

8. Paula Fredriksen, "Passover," *Frontline*. Published April 1998, PBS.org: www.pbs.org/wgbh/pages/frontline/shows/religion/portrait/temple.html (February 18, 2018).

9. R. T. France, *The Gospel of Mark: The New International Greek Testament Commentary* (Grand Rapids: Eerdmans, 2002), 348.

10. "Current or former patients are invited to join the program to be matched with a runner training and fundraising for Boston Children's Hospital. Partners are encouraged to share their Boston Children's journey with their runner to provide them with inspiration and motivation to finish the 26.2 miles! Patients are part of the race day excitement, and are honorary members of the Miles

for Miracles team." "Patient Partners," Boston Children's Hospital: Miles for Miracles: http://fundraise.childrenshospital.org/site/TR?pg=informational&fr_id=1671&type=fr_informational&sid=1017 (April 17, 2018).

11. In Matthew 9:1, Capernaum is described as Jesus' "own town."

12. M. B. Winstead, "Capernaum," *The Lexham Bible Dictionary*, ed. John D. Barry (Bellingham, WA: Lexham Press, 2016).

13. Ibid.

14. Jay Neugeboren, *An Orphan's Tale: A Novel* (New York: Holt Rinehart & Winston, 1976), Kindle edition, location 2344 of 4094.

15. "Jewish Burial Practices," *NIV Archaeological Study Bible*, 1688. See also J. W. Drakeford & E. R. Clendenen, "Grief and Mourning," in C. Brand et al., eds., *Holman Illustrated Bible Dictionary* (Nashville: Holman, 2003), 690–91.

16. Joey Dodson, "A Decisive Rip: Unveiling God's Response to the Death of Jesus," *Bible Study Magazine*, March/April 2018, 6.

17. Craig S. Keener and John H. Walton, eds., *The NIV Cultural Backgrounds Bible: Bringing to Life the Ancient World of Scripture* (Grand Rapids: Zondervan, 2016), note on Matthew 20:20.

18. For more information on dining during Jesus' time, see "Triclinia," *NIV Archeological Study Bible*, 1748.

19. John Nolland, *The Gospel of Matthew: The New International Greek Testament Commentary* (Grand Rapids: Eerdmans, 2005), note on Matthew 20:21.

20. Peter Grier, "How Does Seating at the State of the Union Speech Work?" January 25, 2011. *The Christian Science Monitor*: www.csmonitor.com/USA/Politics/Decoder/2011/0125/How-does-seating-at-the-State-of-the-Union-speech-work (August 9, 2018).

21. "A wedding celebration could last as long as a week, and the financial responsibility lay with the groom (cf. 2:9–10). To run out of supplies would be a dreadful embarrassment in a 'shame' culture; there is some evidence it could also lay the groom open to a lawsuit from aggrieved relatives of the bride." Carson, *Gospel According to John*, note on John 2:3.

22. "The form of address, *gynai* (NIV 'Dear woman'), though thoroughly courteous, is not normally an endearing term, nor the form of address preferred by a son addressing a much-loved mother. When Jesus addresses Mary from the cross, he uses the same expression (19:26)." D. A. Carson, ed. *The Gospel According to John* (Grand Rapids: Eerdmans, 1991), note on John 2:4.

23. Ibid.

24. Ibid., note on John 2:7–8.